ONE DAY IN MARCH

AND

MOVING WITH THE MUSE

BY

BRIGID PATRICIA BOGGAN

Order this book online at www.trafford.com
or email orders@trafford.com

Most Trafford titles are also available at major online book retailers.

Printed in Victoria, BC, Canada.

ISBN: 978-1-4269-2236-7 (sc)

Our mission is to efficiently provide the world's finest, most comprehensive book publishing service, enabling every author to experience success. To find out how to publish your book, your way, and have it available worldwide, visit us online at www.trafford.com

Trafford rev. 12/22/2009

North America & international
toll-free: 1 888 232 4444 (USA & Canada)
phone: 250 383 6864 • fax: 812 355 4082

DEDICATION

This book is dedicated to my dear friends

SISTER CARMEL

MAURA BOYLE ANN O' CONNOR

Introduction

Memories came flooding back for Coventrians on that day in March; when an unexploded German bomb was found during excavations on the new Belgrade Plaza site; resulting in the evacuation of Bonds Court and Bonds Hospital.

The City centre came to a standstill with the disruption of many businesses, such as shops and offices. People remained cheerful and positive throughout the drama. The residents of Bonds were no exception, as some related their remarkable stories of that unforgettable night of the blitz, that devastated Coventry in November 1940, when Hitler's bombs rained down, resulting in a huge loss of life, leaving the City in ruins. Still the people of Coventry were not deterred and it was no different in March 2008.

Brigid concludes her story with her own stroll down memory lane as she moves, once more, with her inspirations of the past and present times.

CHAPTER ONE

One Day In March

March the 12th 2008, began as a normal cold Wednesday. My flat in Bonds Hospital, Hill Street, Coventry was warm and cosy. Ruth and myself were sitting at the table, making amendments to my new book 'NEVER HAD IT SO GOOD.' It was 1.30pm when a quick, sharp knock on my door brought me to my feet. It was our Scheme Manager, Jan. She said, 'Brigid, we have to evacuate the building immediately, a bomb has been found in the area. Put some warm clothing on and will you please collect any medication you may need for this evening and come down quickly to the lounge. We have arranged for some coaches to arrive soon.'

Closing the door, I didn't panic. Turning to Ruth, who had jumped up, and pushing her chair back she said, 'What! A bomb?'

'Oh well,' I replied, 'it's probably a hoax; just get your coat on. Leave everything on the table as it is while I get my medication.' And putting on a warm coat, I locked the door behind me.

We were both soon on our way to the lounge, where most of the residents had assembled. It seemed like the Blitz all over again! All of us wondered where the bomb was found, as we waited for the coaches to arrive, wondering where we were going.

Les, who is our handy man, reassured us saying, 'Don't worry you are all going on a mystery tour of Coventry!'

Our Director, Mrs. Bradford, the Manager, Catriona, and Jan were in attendance, calmly making light of the drama that had happened so quickly and unexpectedly. Some of the residents were out shopping. This was a big responsibility for the Staff, who had to make sure the building was cleared, as well as Bonds Court across the road. Still there was no panic, nobody flapped!

Ruth made her way home through the City centre, where a lot of the roads were blocked off. Shops and offices in Corporation Street and surrounding areas were quickly and efficiently evacuated.

Police and Traffic wardens had everything under control. Reporters from the Evening Telegraph were flitting about with cameras. It was uncanny though, that the Play 'One Night in November' was to be shown that evening in the Belgrade Theatre, close to the scene where the unexploded bomb had been discovered!

The Bomb Squad were immediately alerted. It was chaotic in the City centre. The buses were at a standstill, as most roads were sealed off to traffic, as people made there way home on foot.

The coaches arrived and we were soon boarding amid laughter and a few moans. The mystery tour was a joke of course. We were taken to the Baptist Hall in Earlsdon! One minute I was correcting my Memoir's and the next I was being evacuated for the first time in my life at the ripe old age of 83!

As we travelled on that afternoon in March, Jan was on our coach with book in hand, ticking off all our names as we alighted from the coach and entered the Baptists Hall where the Red Cross and Salvation Army were preparing hot drinks for us, tables and chairs were arranged around the large hall and radiators were switched on, staff from Bond's were with us.

This drama brought back memories to many of our English residents, as they chatted cheerfully and sang all the war time Greats; 'White Cliffs of Dover,' 'We'll Meet Again,' 'Aufweidersen,' reminding me of Vera Lynn and my teens. The courage of these ladies impressed me. I couldn't help but admire their sense of humour.

Again Reporters from the Evening Telegraph were walking about with cameras talking with us and asking what each of us had been doing when we were alerted, as they made notes of our names and ages.

There was also a Representative from the Red Cross sitting at each table, taking details of our Doctor's names and address and what medication we were on etc...

It was about 6pm when we were informed the bomb had not yet been defused and that the situation could go on overnight or even days!

There was a friendly, caring atmosphere surrounding us. Some of the residents that had no relatives in Coventry were taken to Care Homes in the City for the night where they were warmly welcomed. All this was organised by the Staff, who by this time were looking very tired themselves. A Doctor was in attendance to make sure we all had sufficient medication. It was a Doctor from my own Surgery, 'Springfield' on Bennett Road South that was on duty that evening. We were getting more details on the situation as evening wore on, sitting together as the residents related their own experiences of the war that had devastated Coventry, in the early 1940's.

It was fascinating to listen to them; all their stories were so different. In the middle of all the excitement we were told by Staff the bomb had been discovered by workmen on the Belgrade Plaza, where new Hotels and Restaurants were being built. The device was found on the site near the Premier Inn in Upper Well Street. It was 18 inches long and 6 inches in diameter. A no-go zone was widened from 200m to 500m. Thousands of workers were evacuated from their workplace and cars were trapped in car parks!

The bomb was identified as a 50kg German bomb. It was moved and exploded 40 metres from where it was found, at about 3am on Thursday morning, March 13th. A 12ft deep hole was dug to minimize the impact and the bomb was placed in it. A hole was excavated; the bomb was put in the mortar tub and placed inside. Sand bags were used, as well as wooden planks to cover it up. It certainly made a good hole in the ground and lots of bits of wood flew out all over the place. Had it gone off over ground it would have taken out the site! It was a 50kg bomb packed with 22kg explosives!

Spirits were kept high in the Queens Road Baptist Hall near the Butts, by residents of Bonds Hospital as they sang away and waited for overnight accommodation. Maisie Fildes aged 90 spent the night at her granddaughter's house in Bulkington.

She later said, 'I had a sleepless night; I couldn't relax because I wondered if Coventry would explode. I just wanted to come back home and everything would be normal.'

Vera Miles told me her memories of the Blitz and they were as follow: 'Stan and I decided to go to Nuneaton to stay with relations. The factory in Gosford Street where I worked had a direct hit and, as we were getting married in November we decided to go. Stan and his dad cycled each day to Coventry to work. On the night of the Blitz we watched the City burning and wondered what the outcome would be. I thought of my parents, were they ok?'

On the next morning November 16th, my Wedding Day, things looked grim, Stan's step-mum managed to get in touch with a couple of friends who loaned us two cars. We got to Ansty and we found the police stopping the traffic into Coventry.

We told them that we were getting married at 1 pm at St Peters Church in Hillfields.

They said, 'You'll be lucky!! The City is in ruins.'

They let us go as far as Gosford Street and up Swan Lane with great difficulty, to where my parents lived. Mum and Dad were shaken but ok.

Stan and his brother walked to Ball Hill to see if the cars were still available. Yes they were. Mum was worried as we had no food for the reception, only bread and cheese with tea to drink. I was getting ready when a delayed bomb exploded by the Rover Works up the road by the canal in Red Lane.

We made it to the church amid chaos and rubble. Soldiers were clearing up the churchyard and offered to carry myself and the little bridesmaids up to the church.

Reverend Paul Stacey was very surprised to see us. We waited whilst he cleaned himself up and we were married!

We were told that four of Stan's family had been killed in Radford. When we arrived back to Swan Lane my Uncle Wal who had a motor coach took us all back to Nuneaton where Stan had made an arrangement with his relatives to do a surprise meal for all of us. So the day went well after all!

Olive Mason aged 86 was one of the last pensioners to leave the Baptist Hall at midnight on Wednesday. She was taken to St Andrews House in Earlsdon for the night. She said she was looked after very well.

During the war she had lived in Melton Mowbray, they didn't have a Blitz there, so what happened on Wednesday was new to her!

Her neighbour Ken Gibbs aged 80 said, 'Pensioners took the bomb scare in their stride, as they had lived through it all before.' Ken stayed with his daughter in Potters Green.

I stayed the night at my daughter's house in Browns Lane, Allesley. Her husband picked me up at 9.30pm. He had been in the middle of decorating. So I too was comfortable and safe!

Vera Miles felt she was back all those years ago, every night it was bombings and bombings!

'We were so scared we used to sit under the stairs for shelter.'

Vera stayed with her son that night and slept on a water bed.

She said,' I had a good nights sleep in the end; because it was a relief, I knew I was safe!'

The whole City showed great calmness. The Police and the Bomb Squad were excellent in the way they handled every thing during the bomb drama.

The media kept everyone informed while the City was sealed off. People didn't panic, and the City Council made sure everyone was looked after.

The Centre's such as; St Peter's Church Hillfields,

Bablake School and The Queens Road Baptist Hall cared for everyone while Morrison's Supermarket supplied the food.

The pupils at St Osburg's R.C. School in upper Hill Street were evacuated to nearby Bablake School which was in the safe zone. They waited at the school in Coundon for their parents to pick them up. Some parents didn't get there until 5.30pm because they got stuck in traffic as the City Centre came to a standstill!

All things considered the City Centre came through the disruption pretty well. The war in 1940 didn't deter them when Hitler's bomb's rained down, and it was no different in 2008!

The team work of the Coventry Telegraph was excellent, conducting interviews and gathering exclusive pictures, also production of their paper, despite the bomb being on their doorstep in Corporation Street. They evacuated the building; still they brought their paper out with every detail. Not forgetting the Staff at Bonds Hospital and Bonds Court, who carried out their duty in a very sensitive and caring way. Well done to all of you!

The West Midlands Police thanked the Residents and Business people of Coventry for their support following the discovery of an unexploded World War 2 incendiary device in the City Centre on that memorable day in March 2008.

The Play, 'One Night In November' recalling the 1940's will now return to the Belgrade Theatre later this year.

Some of this detailed information regarding the size and position of the device found in Well Street on March 12th was taken from The Coventry Telegraph ON FRIDAY, MARCH 14TH 2008.

July 16th 2008 is rather a changeable breezy day after a sunny morning. 'It's the famous Strawberry Tea' occasion here at Bond's Hospital and because of the weather it's held in our lovely Lounge. The several tables scattered around are colourful and tastefully set out.

This year the event was very special, marked by the naming of the Lounge. The Plaque was unveiled by our oldest resident, Olive Green.

It was one of the Trustees that came up with the name at one of their Meetings. So it is now called:

'The Walter Keene Lounge.'

Olive Green spoke about the Almshouses small beginnings in a very descriptive and moving way.

Walter Keene was born on August 26th 1903 in Leicester into a family with a tradition of Public Service. His father was High Sheriff of Leicester and his elder brother Sir Charles Keene served as Lord Mayor. He married Mary in 1928 and moved to Coventry to open a branch of the family retail and Financial Business.

He spent his life in the service of others having been at various times a Group Scout Master, Sunday School Superintendent, a Methodist Circuit Steward and for over 70years a Methodist local Preacher. He played his part in the life of the City becoming Chairman of the Retail Section of the Chamber of Commerce in 1964 and Chairman of Coventry Savings Committee for 8 years from 1966, for which he received the MBE. He was President of the Rotary Club of Coventry in 1958, founding President of

The Coventry Probus Club and became National President of his Trade Federation in 1967.

He was for many years involved in the Council of Churches and was a Trustee of the Chapel of Unity. He was a member of Trinity Lodge of Freemasons No. 254 for 63 years.

In 1961 he was appointed a Trustee of Coventry Church and (Municipal) Charities which manages the Tudor Almshouses of Ford's and Bond's Hospitals. He became Chairman in 1964 and under his leadership a major Programme of improvement and development began. He retired in 1990.

Walter died 20th July 1998, shortly after his 95th Birthday and his 70th Wedding Anniversary. He was greatly respected by all who knew him as one who spent a lifetime in the service of God and his fellow men.

The unveiling of the Plaque was toasted with Champagne.

> How proud and honoured Bond's Hospital
> must be today to name their Lounge after this
> REMARKABLE man Walter Keene.

And so our celebrations continued on this special day of the 'Strawberry Tea.'

We had live music provided by 2 Disc Jockeys. It was very nostalgic and as usual the Residents swayed and sang to the music.

Our Director Carol Bradford and all The Scheme Managers waited on us and the long serving tables were adorned with delicious home made cakes and dainties, along with a large square iced cake made by Mrs Bradford herself. In addition to all this were large bowls of raspberries and strawberries with fresh cream.

Les our Handyman, also the important cleaning ladies were helping to make a fuss of us.

The Trustees were well in attendance and visited all the tables to chat with us. It was so obvious to see how much they were enjoying seeing us together and happy. What dedicated people they are, it seems their work is never done, ensuring we are secure and comfortable in their wonderful Almshouses!

I can't even imagine what it involves to keep everything in the Almshouses running smoothly. It was indeed intriguing to listen to our Chairman Mr Keene's opening speech, (who is incidentally the son of Walter Keene and following in his remarkable father's footsteps!) He described how the Almshouses first began in small bed sits, with only room enough for single iron bedsteads, liking to what one saw in the old Hospitals, with only cast iron grates for cooking and heating.

How proud the Trustees must be today entering Bond's Hospital and Bond's Court, and still planning more buildings in time to come. It seems there is no end to their work, and the great people behind them. There are no words to express our appreciation of what we are now enjoying from their tireless efforts!

I am convinced somebody knelt and prayed the morning I walked into Bond's Hospital to apply for a flat. And the gentleman I followed in turned and said to me, 'You're on camera you know! You should not have followed me in!'

Not being familiar with the security regulations, I wondered what he meant. Then thankfully, the office door opened and a lady greeted me, handing me an appointment card for my application and hence the happy ending! We are all just passing through but Bond's will go on until the end of Time!

Staff at Bond's Hospital being presented with the 'Investors in people' award on 20th August 2009

SHARING A GLIMPSE OF A WINTER SCENE IN SPRINGTIME

Looking out the window on Sunday, April 6th 2008, our courtyard here at Bonds was magnificent following a heavy snow fall. No postcard could describe it sufficiently. The tall, bare branches of the trees were covered with snow; together with the roofs of the 15th Century buildings and St Johns Church. The sun now peeping through slowly began to melt the snow as it fell in soft flakes to the ground. A car dotted here and there in the yard with white windows and roofs. It truly was spectacular!

Just having put my soda bread into the oven, I took time to gaze through my kitchen window and pen this beautiful and unusual scene in April. Taking me back to the 30's in December. Unfortunately I didn't have a film in my camera to snap it. It feels so good to be alive this beautiful morning and witness something so unique in springtime!

One could never imagine that just beyond St John's Church is the centre of Coventry City and Medieval Spon Street!

A few people came through the gates with cameras, no doubt to catch the splendour of the show which disappeared all too soon with the heat of the sun!

BOOK LAUNCH AT BONDS

August 30th 2008. It's Launch Night for my new book, 'NEVER HAD IT SO GOOD'. I've had a busy morning in preparation. It's holiday time and I am just hoping that not too many people will be away. The sun is shining this morning and it's warm here in Coventry. The timer has just buzzed to remind me my baking is complete. I hope it tastes as good as it looks.

I am more organised and relaxed this time for the occasion, maybe I am getting used to being an Author! It can be a bit overwhelming. Tom will entertain us once more with the accordion music, so popular with our residents.

Maggie Gallagher is attending with a few of her dance team. She is a family friend and a very talented girl. Mags and my granddaughter Deborah are taking care of all the preparations. Annie is away on holiday in Ireland right now. Ruth will arrange the table for my books, put up balloons etc. And display the Coventry and Irish flag, (which was supplied by the Irish Centre in Hill Street) Kate, Paula, and the great-grandchildren are looking forward to the occasion.

Deborah will sit with me as I do the signing. Bill and Sean (Deborah's husband) will be on the door, making sure there is no breach of security. It does take a lot of organising. However; the important thing is that everyone enjoy themselves.

The Chairman, Mr Keene opened the Launch and spoke very well on my behalf. I was surprised when Mr Brendan Farrell a Reporter from the Irish Post arrived for a story on the book and took some photographs. The Irish dancers performed beautifully and my great-granddaughter Alana danced solo. So all went well and it was an exciting night.

On the 15th September, 2008 my friend Rose Lynch took me to Saint Bernard's Abbey and Monastery near Leicester. It was a bright sunny day. The Monastery is off the beaten track, an avenue of leafy trees lined the driveway to the entrance. It was built in the 1800's and set in beautiful surroundings, with magnificent views.

We arrived in time for 8.am Mass; it was a very moving experience. Several Priests presided together with the Monks.

Rose drew my attention to the sunrise as we proceeded to the Dining room for breakfast. This was fascinating to watch, as it actually changed colours and appeared to dance. We enjoyed our meal together with a few people that were on Retreat from London for the weekend.

We met Father Laurence; I think he is Nigerian, a very happy charismatic character. We did a tour of the Abbey's; bedrooms, rest rooms and sitting rooms. The silence and spirituality of the place was very impressive.

After breakfast we went to the Grotto and recited the Rosary. It was the Feast of Our Lady of Sorrows. Then we did the Steps to Calvary, before going back to the Abbey to visit the beautiful book store, where we purchased some nice cards and leaflets. It was a lovely day and an unforgettable experience. I look forward to going on a few days Retreat in the spring. It's as special to me as Lourdes and Medjugorge, except that it is on my doorstep, an hour's drive from Coventry. I'm told most people in Leicestershire are totally unaware of this little paradise. I feel so privileged to have experienced the stillness and sanctity of the Monastery.

CHAPTER TWO

Waterford, the Crystal County where I was born, is known as the 'Sunny South East.' The City stands on the River Suir. For many years it has been a very busy Seaport. During the 18th Century the Industry of the City prospered and is famous world wide for its Crystal glass.

It has a very ancient Harbour and the Cargo boats are still coming and going. It is still one of Ireland's busiest Ports.

The Museum on the Quay provides fascinating information into the lives of Waterford's Viking and Norman ancestors; it is believed to be one of Ireland's oldest Cities.

From the Museum you can do a tour along the Plaza which was built to celebrate the Millennium year. It is dedicated to William Vincent Wallace, famous for his wonderful Operas, 'Maratana,' and 'Lurin.' He is one of the greatest Composers of English Opera.

Reginald's Tower is the oldest Civic building in Ireland. It has stood on the corner of the Mall for over 1.000 years. It protected the City in earlier days from invasion.

A visit to the Glass Factory is well worth while and it is fascinating to watch the skilful Blowers at work, shaping the glass into pieces of wonderful art. The chandeliers they produce are magnificent.

The Seaside Town of Tramore is famous for its 3 mile beach and the 'Metal Man' – those with romance in mind we are told by Irish Folklore, should hop around the base of the 'Metal Man' three times and they are assured to be married within the year!

The City boasts of so many varied Restaurants and Pub meals, one is spoiled for choice. I can't forget to mention Dunmore East, a beautiful picturesque village.

It is situated at the entrance of Waterford Harbour. Indeed it's now a very different City to the one I remember in the late 1930's and early 40's.

- The Clock Tower, Waterford

Its wonderful now on visits back home to see so many improvements and make a comparison of then and now! When I was young, the class distinction that separated us from the swanks was very obvious. Theirs were the better off houses with linoleumed floors, smelling of furniture polish, and the aroma of toast and tea brewing on Sunday mornings. Breakfast for them, consisted of rashers and sausages.

If we were lucky, we had fried bread sprinkled with salt and maybe porridge. Blaa's were a great treat purchased from Roach's Bakery in the Glen. They were crusty and round, resembling the batches of today but tasted delicious, while still warm from the oven. The shop opened at 8.30am in the mornings and there was always a queue waiting. Those Blaa's cost a penny each and could be bought in batches of six or even a dozen for large families. Roach's were open six days a week; it was a very popular Bakery.

Waterford being a seaport town, the men waited at the docks the days the boats came in. Sometimes they were hand picked and many turned away. This meant there was no food for the week for those families. They survived by helping each other out. That gesture was common amongst the poor.

Coal and slack were sold and weighed out at the Water-side off John's Street in Waterford and was mostly collected by women and pushed home on the push bike or rolled in wheelbarrows. There were coal deliveries, but the very poor collected their own!

Dan Sheedy's was the Pawn Broker on the Hill of Ballybricken. The shop had 3 brass balls over the front door and always a few people waiting outside. Especially on a Monday morning, including myself aged about 11. I would be standing with my little parcel tied with twine and clutched to my chest helping to keep me warm. It contained Daddy's trousers or jacket.

Waiting for a neighbour to come along and take it into the shop for me. Telling her 'Daddy said,' Will you please ask for 4/-, as he will probably 'cut' you anyway, he usually does. But we will redeem it Friday when we get the Dole.'

She would answer me saying! 'Alright Brigid Alana.'

It was often foggy and sometimes raining and miserable on those mornings in wintertime. I would be looking forward to arriving home to the slice of hot toast Daddy promised to have waiting for me.

Usually his face fell when I said, 'Mrs Rooney could only get 2/6d!'

Then I would be sent to the shop across the road for a half pound of margarine and a sliced Pan.

I was often late for school that morning, and breathless on arriving in the middle of morning prayers. The Nun always remarked, 'It's Brigid O'Hara late again on a Monday morning!'

How I wished she didn't stress Monday in case the girls in the class guessed I was in Sheedy's. I'm glad it is a misty past now!

During the late 30's and early 40's things were scarce and items were rationed. We were allowed a certain amount of bread, butter, sugar etc... We kids went off sugar for Lent. Most stayed off it! Home made bread was the norm because the loaf available in the shops was a horrible brown half baked thing. Despite the hardship and often pangs of hunger, we were happy and contented with our lot.

The smoke bellowed from the chimneys in our street on cold winter nights when we played in gangs, carefree, so unaware of anything that was going on outside that space of time. People were very poor, some more than others. A lot of children were in their bare feet, sitting on the pavement outside their homes, perhaps enjoying thick slices of bread and jam which they may have got from an neighbour for running an errand.

We often made swings on the poles which were on the pathway outside our houses in the street. The rope was doubled and wound around the pole, pulling the two loose ends through until they dangled, then knotted tightly to make a secure seat to sit on. Then pushing both feet against the pole, we swung high into the air and round and round we went. Each of us taking turns for our swings. Then there were the skipping ropes and racing hoops, which we chased with sticks along the road. These were mostly old bicycle wheels which had the spikes removed.

Just simple activities, yet we were so unaware how healthy those games really were. Great exercise keeping us fit. We also had running competitions, eventually going to bed so tired but relaxed with our cup of cocoa.

My first job at the age of 11 was in a big house on the Mall in the City. My work entailed cleaning the stairs, dusting the furniture, and shaking the mats from the long hallway. It was early Saturday morning. Mammy would take me by the hand to Mrs O'Toole's door, telling her she would collect me later. I was given my dinner there and 2 shillings for the days work. Then Mammy came to collect me in the evening. And on the way home she bought bread, margarine, and sugar with my wages.

Looking back now, I think that was so sad for Mammy who had gone from riches to rags!

Bubbles, one of my sisters (and she WAS a little bubbles too), though could be fiery. She made her First Holy Communion in two odd plimsolls! One black and one white! Mam spent the night before, applying layers of whitening to the black canvas, hoping it wouldn't rain on the day! Thankfully it didn't rain but when Bubbles knelt at the Altar rails with rows of the other children, she had one black and one white sole of the shoes showing! I wonder how Mam felt looking on, as she knelt in the Church pews, behind the child. Fortunately Bubbles was unaware, and to make the incident more poignant, the Church was filled with the voices of those little 'angels,' boys and girls, as they approached the Altar singing, 'Jesus thou art coming, Holy as thou art, thou the God who made me, to my sinful heart….'

Today I am happy to say, Bubbles lives in England with her family and husband of 50 years. She is very happy and comfortable but more importantly, is still bubbly!

What a comparison this is to today's children making their First Holy Communion. With dresses costing £100 and sometimes even more, and cars waiting to take them to Hotels for Receptions. Often equal to those of Weddings! Yet I'm sure Bubbles and Mammy both sat and laughed that evening, recalling the black and white plimsoll, way back in the '40's! An excellent description of then and now! That incident can still bring tears to my eyes, for Mammy and my sister as I recall the hymn 'Blessed are you poor, for the Kingdom shall be yours, Blessed are you who weep and mourn, for one day you shall laugh.

I never remember vandalism or loitering. The biggest offence I recall was if a lad stole a bicycle lamp and that was considered very serious. The Gardai would be alerted! And if the lads kicked a ball on the road, it often hit a window or landed in somebody's garden.

Knocking at doors and running away was another bit of devilment that kids got up to, and was very annoying.

Those kind of pranks always existed but generally children were easily controlled and corrected. There was always discipline in the home and rules to abide by, even though there were large families, they usually had a healthy fear of their parents. I recall my father saying,

'If you can't get respect through love, then get it through fear but make sure you get it!' Yet I can't remember him raising his hand to any of us children!

When I was about 16 I had my first lesson in discipline, being all dressed up and ready to go out and meet my friend Mary. Daddy stood in the hallway looking at me very seriously and, pointing to the bolt on the front door,

he said; 'Now my lady, you do see that bolt. It will be well and truly locked at 11pm tonight! Is that clear?

'Yes daddy it is.'

'Right, off you go now and remember, don't walk the Quay side as there will be boats in and it's dangerous.'

On the way home that particular night, Mary and myself were delayed in Delacato's Fish and Chip Shop in John's Town. It was very popular so there were always queues there, with lots of conversation going on between us about the coming attractions in the Regal or Savoy Cinemas. Or maybe the dances and the Big Band sounds expected in the Olympia Ballroom. Always the highlight of our week!

Arriving home at 11.20pm and sure enough the door was locked; I made my way to Mary's house which thankfully was only a 10 minute walk away. I did however learn my first lesson in discipline that night, way back in 1940.

I loved when I walked through our gate to go out in the evenings, leaving the house full of children and noise behind. Especially in the winter time with the smell of chimney smoke and the street lights just a soft glow. Most of the front doors were closed except for a few. The houses were terraced making it convenient for the women to chat over the fence.

I remember when I passed one evening, overhearing Mrs Rooney say, 'Lord save us and Bless us, isn't Brigid growing up fast. She'll soon be ready to fly the nest.'

I hummed as I went along 'A Nightingale sang in Berkeley Square!'

The family circle was very important; we always sat around the table for our meals. Even though we argued between ourselves, often complaining, 'She or he got more than me.' But at least we were talking and in conversation. The fireside was also a place that attracted us as we told ghost stories, often frightening each other and laughing.

When I was a girl at school, many of my companions received physical punishment, often severe, from teachers who were entrusted with our education and welfare. And if they brought the fact to the attention of their parents, they risked more punishment from them, for giving the teacher trouble at school. So it was a no win situation!

I remember school assembly in the early 30's; each class was lined up in single file, where we all marched to our different classrooms ready for Roll call at 9am. We began with morning prayers, followed by English and Irish lessons. Then we had the (green) Catechism.

Our lunch break was only 30 minutes. Just enough time to eat our packed lunch and have 10 minutes play time. Occasionally the extremely poor children would be sent discreetly to the kitchen of the Convent for their meal.

In the afternoon we were taught knitting and sewing, cookery, choir practice and P.E. (physical education). These subjects were our usual timetable.

A Gardai called to the school to check the Roll book and if there was absenteeism, it was reported to the school Inspector, who then informed the parents.

Children were warned by parents and Teachers, if they got lost, to always ask a Gardai (who was usually on foot patrol or on his push bike) for directions. There were no cars for the Gardai's in those days, except in the case of a serious crime, which was seldom.

It was common practice for the nuns, after school hours, to visit the sick and the elderly in their homes. They also had to do the marking of the pupil's homework in the evening. Their schedules were very busy, as they had many different duties in the Convent.

These were the times when parents and teachers were always right, and children were to be seen and not heard. We respected our parents, teachers, and the Law. Personally I don't regret any of it. Sometimes I admit, at school it did seem harsh and unfair, and maybe even going too far. Now it has swung much too far the other way! Parents and teachers are often afraid of the children, whose attitude is, 'If you hit me I will report you to the Authorities.' What a sad world it is now! But of course there is always the exception. There are still some very nice, helpful teenagers. Except for the ones who spoil it for the majority, mostly now we hear 'Me, me, me.' 'I want,' 'I'm bored.' If you notice, life is a constant struggle, and continual tension about what I want and what I need!

We can only speculate on the cause of their emotional disturbance. But isn't it likely that the breakdown in society, is a contributory factor.

In Doncaster recently, there was shocking news where two boys aged 9 and 11, were attacked and suffered terrible injuries. Many young children in our society are so consumed with rage that it has to be expressed in violence. Too many children are deprived of their right to grow up in a loving, secure home.

The current preferred adult lifestyle is a succession of father figures passing through the household. Most of whom have no affection or interest in them. It appears that mothers and fathers put their own search for happiness over the interest of their children, with predictable consequences which we now see.

The extreme violence on television and computer screens encourages them to imitate. It would appear that the Doncaster crime is just one example of the results.

Teachers are being forced to cope with disruptive pupils every day. Imposing discipline on children can be very difficult. If a teacher attempts to punish a child for bad behaviour, the response of the parent is far too often to take the child's side, by attacking the professional verbally or even physically.

A little girl aged about 6 said to me before Christmas last year, 'I'm getting a present from Santa for £100 and my Brother, (who incidentally was younger) is getting the same.'

I couldn't help thinking how sad that the value of this present was immediately emphasised by this young child. This wonderful season of Christmas is now so materialistic; the real meaning of the season is forgotten!

What is happening to the society that we live in. It's now a world of THINGS where the generations are getting wiser but weaker. How often do we hear it suggested that we should indulge our every whim and desire? This means we are not free; our hearts are filled with worldly wisdom. It would appear that God has been removed from our lives, when he is actually immersed in them. Just imagine depending on ourselves alone with no-one to turn to, surely then we are lost!

Despite the hardship that I remember as a child, I do feel I owe my parents a lot for the love they gave, the burdens we shared together and above all for the faith they handed down to me. Prayer was part of their daily lives and when death came it was accepted, with the assurance we would all meet in heaven one day!

Now it seems to be moving towards a 'Godless Society.' It's all about making money and having a good time.

Parents have a huge responsibility in guiding their children. It is vital to implant values that form their character. Some parents don't know or care what their children do. Then we have the ones that will control but are not allowed to.

There are so many ways to discipline. So where do we begin? I believe it has to start in the home and school. With communities getting together, I'm sure we all have a part to play.

The home and family are the very foundation of life. Now there are few marriages, young girls having two and three children most of them not knowing who the fathers are! How sad that is for the children with a background such as this. With no stability one wonders what will become of these children. Who are getting one message from one place and getting another from another place. There has to be a balance. Teenagers often pick up negative attitudes from society, so it has to be structured by communities making an effort to come together. It is probably a good idea to look in the mirror and think what we can do!

It's almost unbelievable that the latest news on the 'Acts of Parliaments' is that some MP's are trying to have a new Law passed whereby teenagers can actually walk into their Doctors Surgeries and have abortions, and they suggest that Midwives and Nurses could also perform abortions! This is beyond comprehension.

One wonders what these people are thinking about. As abortion can have a very serious affect on the mother in later years, both physically and mentally.

If this Law is passed 'God forbid,' surely their own intelligence should tell them this is very wrong. Where have our moral standards gone?

This surely is encouraging teenagers instead of deterring them!

I read an article in a book a priest wrote one time, it went as follows:

> *'If you ever waken up one morning and life is like what you always wanted it to be, then don't move, stay right where you are and wait 'til the Undertaker arrives!'*

I love this well expressed thought on life, I am sure you will too!

CHAPTER THREE

The Countryside

Our countryside was very different from the City and Towns. I remember visiting Kilmacow near Waterford in my teens. It's just like a dream now and fascinating to recall the lazy, hazy days of summer, after the apple blossom had blown from the trees and with the encouragement of the sun, the fruits beginning to ripen in their place.

Then there was autumn with the leaves turning to gold! Leaving the City behind and cycling along Sallypark with its rows of small terraced houses. Neighbours in conversation waved as you passed by.

Gradually you entered the countryside, with its big fields and grassy ditches on either side. It was peaceful as traffic dwindled down, you were likely though to be confronted by a herd of cattle being driven towards you by the farmer and you had to dismount and almost lean against the ditch on the narrow road to allow the cattle to pass. The farmer's salute was usually, 'Good day to you.'

Manure and new mown hay was a familiar smell in the Country and could be overpowering, yet the air was crisp and fresh, you realized how wonderful nature is.

In the autumn time there are fields of corn, and when the wind blows the corn bends low. Then when the wind has gone it finds its own poise and balance again.

Creativity is also an example of this, with its flexible and measured tensions. The violin for instance, if the strings are tuned too tightly or too loosely they snap, but with the tuning balanced the violin produces powerful and wonderful music. All these pleasant thoughts come to mind as you cycle along the countryside in Ireland. Memory is a great friend of solitude, you never forget the impressions they leave.

In some parts of Ireland it is believed that the dead do not live far away; their ghosts are often reported to be seen in old ruins and fields. At least so Celtic tradition tells us!

When I was young I heard stories of the 'Fairy Coach' that travelled through the country villages on dark windy nights. And the dogs hearing the noise followed the coach until it crashed and then there was dead silence! The Bean Si' ('Si' means fairies)! This fairy woman wails or cries in the area where someone is about to die. My mother-in-law claimed to have often heard this spirit cry and sure enough someone in that neighbourhood did die.

I recall finding all this very intriguing and entertaining. The country side is full of wonder and haunting stories. It is said, when we die and the last thread of our life is finally cut, our loved ones that have gone before us will come to meet us as we journey home.

There is also a strong belief in the use of Holy Water as the soul departs, and of course it is still used at funerals today.

An old lady once told me that if there was any disharmony in her family home her mother would sprinkle Holy Water, as she believed any disquiet did not come from God and she would tell the devil to go to hell, as he was the only person you could tell to go to hell! I think that makes a lot of sense!

To add to the charm of autumn there was the Threshing that took place at the end of August or early September, when the corn was gathered from the fields. A very busy and exciting time for the farmers! The women folk got busy in the kitchens preparing the food. Several barrels of 'porter' stood ready for the celebrations to follow.

The corn was put through the thresher where all the wheat was extracted and saved in large sacks, leaving just the straw. This was then gathered and taken to the barns, making warm bedding for the animals.

With the threshing finished the celebrations began, as all the neighbouring farmers gathered in one of the farmhouses, sharing the porter from the barrels and enjoying a sing-song that went on into the early hours of the morning.

Life in the country was very relaxed and laid back and enhanced by the furnishings in the farmhouse. So in keeping with the simple life there was the old fashioned dresser, where jugs and tins of every description took their place and the large enamelled teapot surrounded with all sorts of everything old. As the day drifted into evening the fading sunlight streamed through the half open door, with the old dog stretched on the ground enjoying the sun that was warming her., Sometimes it seemed those lazy afternoons went on forever and so different to the bustle of the City.

In the mornings the farmer prepared for the days work ahead as he tackled up the horse and cart in the farmyard, getting ready for Market day. The horse trotted along the country roads to the City, perhaps to the Flour Mills where the farmer collected the flour, which was so important on the farm for the bread making, and to purchase whatever household necessities were needed. The country folk were self sufficient in many things, such as;

vegetables of all kinds, fruits, eggs, bacon, milk and of course the butter which they churned themselves, (keeping the women folk very busy)! Buttermilk was plentiful and was used to make the soda bread. It always fascinated me to watch Molly in Twomey's mix the soda bread; this was like second nature to her.

In a large bowl she mixed the ingredients which consisted of; flour, bi-carbonate of soda and a little salt. She then added buttermilk until she had combined sticky dough. Leaving the bowl almost clean she tipped the dough onto a floured scrubbed table, then kneaded it for about 3 minutes, shaping it into a round, and with a knife made a cross on the top of the dough, transferring it to a large cast iron pot that hung from a hook over the fire. Putting the lid back on the pot and using large tongs, Molly covered the lid with the hot coals and turf. After what seemed about an hour and a half this beautiful soda bread was removed from the pot and the bottom of the bread was tapped to make sure it had a hollow sound, which meant the bread was ready! Then it was wrapped in a tea towel, while the steam softened the crust.

The bread was placed on the table and allowed to cool, resting on its side ready for tea time. It would then be cut up and served with country butter and an assortment of home-made jams. As you can imagine, I always enjoyed my tea at the farm and can still taste that delicious soda bread.

Seamus Duffy was a farmhand that Twomey's employed. And as he worked away, he always sang the same tune; consequently I had the song off by heart. It was the famous 'Rose of Tralee!'

> 'The pale moon was rising above the Blue Mountains; the sun was declining beneath the blue sea. The moon o'er the valley its pale rays were spreading when I won the heart of the Rose of Tralee.
> She was lovely and fair, like the rose of the summer but it was not her beauty alone that won me.

Oh no, 'twas the truth in her eyes ever dawning,
that made me love Mary, the Rose of Tralee.'

The fields around the farms were always lush and green. Nothing appears to change over the years. This peace and tranquillity always existed in the heart of the Country where time seems to stands still! The conversation between the country folk was mostly about the animals; the cows and the sheep and the geese in the leafy orchard.

I loved the thatched roofs of the farmhouses, the old fashioned roses with tiny buds growing beside the half door and the bees humming around them. Everything seemed to be caught up in the slow movement of time as the old kitchen clock ticked away.

The faithful old sheepdog still sleeping and dreaming, (one wonders about what) in the peace and stillness and the fading light of the evening, all so immersed in the natural surroundings of the countryside.

Reluctantly on one of those early summer evenings in the 1940's, I would cycle back to Waterford along the quiet winding country roads, with the smell of the wild flowers enveloping me, I often found myself humming Seamus Duffy's favourite tune.

On arriving home, daddy overhearing me, would remark, 'you've been to Kilmacow again?'

I can't talk about the countryside without a mention of the 'Barn' and 'Cross Road' Dances. They provided great entertainment for the local lads and lassies to include us 'Townies' when we cycled to them in the summer evenings.

The country girls could be seen in groups, cycling together on the roads, with suitable dance shoes tied to the handlebars of their bikes, often singing that well loved song, 'She Moved through the Fair'!

The Barn Dances were mostly held in the autumn time in out houses, as these were enclosed, and often a good 'hooley' after a wedding was enjoyed there.

The Cross Roads dance floor was a concrete surface. The air was filled with the sound of fiddlers and melodeon box players, often accompanied by a lad playing a mouth organ to harmonize. Passers by in the nearby villages joined the dancers in the evening, until the rising of the moon! I'm sure a lot of Irish dance lovers; my age, can still remember, as their mind flickers back to those bygone wholesome days!

The 'Old-Time Waltz' never went out of fashion; 'The Siege of Ennis' was also popular, whatever the dance there was no effort put into learning it. We just seemed to drift in to the rhythm and danced the night away.

That popular tune 'I Could Have Danced All night' certainly would have applied to our age group when we danced all night in the moonlight. Although the days of wine and roses are short lived, they are still wonderful to recall. To get back from dreaming to reality and the real world, at least it can't take our dreams. They help to soften the hard knocks as we travel through life remembering!

I hope my older readers are romantics, and enjoy looking back with me in their twilight years. Though I do cry at the sad times, I still laugh heartily about the silly things I did along the way.

Preparing to go to a Barn dance one night in late autumn, I vividly remember rolling an old pair of nylon stockings to make two pads and tacking them into the bodice of my dress. At the age of 16 not many of us teenagers were well endowed. The year was 1941.

My dance partner that night was a well built young farmer aged about 18. He wore hob-nailed boots. I wondered if he forgot to change them before leaving for the dance. The sparks were flying from his heels as he swung me rather roughly around the floor. One of my nylon pads came undone, and falling to the ground it got caught in the lace of Conor's boot. When the dance finished, he looked down and said, 'Where's that come from?' Looking innocently back at him, I said, 'I don't know! What is it?'

Trish Maloney was standing beside me and I asked her if she had lost something, as I pointed to Conor's boots.

Indignantly she said,' No I haven't, what's that?'

Conor picked it up and the nylon dangled from his hand. I stood rigid with my arms folded across my chest in case anyone noticed the sagging bodice of my dress, and eventually escaping out into the field to pull the other pad out I threw it over the ditch. Then going back inside, no one noticed as the dance by this time was in full swing, and sadly so was the bodice of my dress!

CHAPTER FOUR

Another memory I have, is of the summers spent in Dunmore East with my auntie and little cousins. They rented a cottage every year for the school holidays.

One particular year stands out in my mind. I was aged about 11 and always helped Auntie with the children. She had 5 little ones then, the eldest would be 6 years old. He was bold and cheeky and he would fight with me if he didn't get his own way, and often kicked me in the shins. Fortunately he would be wearing soft plimsolls resembling the ones of today. In fact we all wore the same; we called them sand shoes and got a new pair each for the holidays.

Every Saturday night I cleaned them using an old toothbrush to apply the whitening, which was sold in small blocks and crumbled into a powder when mixed with cold water. There were 6 pairs to be cleaned up for Mass on Sundays.

I don't remember it ever raining those summers! During the week I would climb the cliffs to reach the farm and collect buttermilk, eggs and country butter for auntie, as she baked a lot of soda bread, potato cakes and apple tarts. Potato cakes were delicious eaten hot and enjoyed with country butter.

Lawlor's pub was popular; Uncle Matt enjoyed his pint there. The beach beside it was called Lawlor's Strand. Over the rocks and under the cliffs there was Councellers Strand. This was more private and the children had more freedom, as they paddled in the water and played with their little buckets and spades, making castles and digging holes in the sand to make puddles and splash each other.

The youngest child was only 12 months old. That same year he was Christened in the Cathedral in Waterford, and I was proud to be his godmother!

A couple of weeks into the holiday, unfortunately I had a nosebleed. This was something I was prone to! However, this one seemed to go on for hours, causing problems for my Auntie. She laid me flat on my back in the cool grass, outside the cottage. She then put blotting paper under my tongue and a bunch of keys down my back, I had both hands in an enamel basin filled with cold water, which she placed either side of me on the grass.

With a cold wet flannel across my forehead, she assured me all this procedure would help to stop the bleeding.

Little James looking down on me wide eyed said,

'If you get better, I will never kick you again!'

I was very frightened seeing all the blood; I prayed silently, 'Jesus please help me?'

Auntie was very concerned for me. She was soon joined by Uncle Matt. He stood by, calmly smoking his pipe. She whispered something into his ear and he nodded in agreement (alarm bells). I thought, I'm bleeding to death and they are sending for the Priest. My eyes were the only part of me that was moving as I took in everything that was going on around me. I felt so tired and weak; I fell asleep on the grass. When I woke up, the towels and the basins had been taken away.

I felt dizzy as Uncle Matt helped me up and we went back to the cottage where I had a glass of cold milk, which I had collected from the farm that day, and the thick cream was floating on the top of the glass. Auntie remarked, 'She needs it now to regain all that blood she has lost!'

James said I looked like a ghost, and frightened him. I drank lots of milk in the days that followed. Sometimes she put Guinness in the milk to build me up. It didn't taste nice, but did the trick of putting the colour back in my cheeks.

I recovered well before returning to Waterford, and school once again.

So maybe the blotting paper and keys weren't a bad idea after all!

Another old remedy I recall is a poultice of bread which had been soaked in boiling water, tossed on to a bandage, some times made from a strip of cotton torn from an old pillow case or sheet and applied quickly while still very hot. To a very painful infection called a whitlow. (Which tended to develop at the side of our fingernails). They were very common and painful, but that bread poultice drew all the pus from the whitlow, or indeed any infection that set in from a cut or wound.

Lifebuoy soap softened and mixed with sugar was another remedy used to draw out infections.

An old sock filled with warm salt and wound around the neck was soothing to a sore throat.

Beef tea was a popular tonic and recommended, particularly to those with tuberculosis.

Guinness mixed with milk was prescribed as a tonic for anaemic patients.

Simple remedies that worked very well and without side effects!

I remember a shop in Barrack Street owned by Daddy Curtis, a little white haired man. His shop was stocked with home remedies. These had a cure for almost everything under the sun, from babies to old age. The shop smelled of herbs and paraffin oil.

Across the road was Thompson's, The Undertakers and is still there to this day.

So many of the old shops in the City come to mind, now replaced with more modern ones; Penny's Store replaces Woolworth's near the Cathedral. Close to that was the Marble Hall, an exclusive Butchers shop The three brothers serving wore flat topped straw hats, and were known as the 'three wise men'.

Further on up was Flannigan's Fish and Poultry shop. Garragins Tobacconist, then the Home and Colonial Grocers. Across the road was The Savoy Cinema with its lovely Restaurant. Further along was the London and Newcastle, a high class Grocery Store; Burton's on the corner of Patrick's Street next, Fitzgerald's exclusive Gents Wear, Boyce's Fashion Shop, Greer's Confectioners, (this shop is situated in the same place today and still standing). These are but a few of the shops in Broad Street that I remember.

Wouldn't it be wonderful if someone came up with the idea to make a film of Waterford as it was back then in the 30's, 40's, and 50's! One song that was composed about Waterford was called 'My City of Music,' and I think that describes our City beautifully!

The Old Quayside, the Docks, the famous Fair Days of Ballybricken, the Dispensary, so valuable to the poorer people of the City, when they queued up for their prescribed medicines, taking their own ketchup bottles, which they handed into the Dispenser through a little hatch in the wall. This hatch was then closed as they waited patiently, for their name to be called. And the medicine handed back, labelled with patients name and instructions. Medicines were mostly iron tonics which were handed out to everybody!! One would have to assume we were all anaemic!

The way your condition was diagnosed by the Doctor at the Dispensary was to gently pull your lower eyelid down and tell you to look towards the ceiling, then he looked at your tongue and without any further comment he wrote a prescription out!

Happily things are different today.

The Doctors in Private Practice resided on The Mall. These were Doctors' Higgins, McCarthy and Dr O'Keeffe, whom I have good reason to remember, because he performed his first Gall Bladder Operation in St. Patrick's Hospital, John's Hill. The patient was in fact myself, I was aged 27 and the year was 1952!

Dr Shannahan also comes vividly to mind. He was very good looking and as I waited in Theatre to be put to sleep, both Dr O'Keeffe and himself were studying the x-ray by the window and I could hear them quite plainly as they discussed the procedure to follow. They both approached me as I waited on the Operating Table, and as the mask was placed over my face, smiling broadly Dr O'Keeffe said, 'Go off to sleep now Brigid and dream about Dr Shannahan!'

Visiting me next morning accompanied by Staff Nurse Louie Ryan, Dr O'Keeffe said, 'Brigid you had enough Stones in there to build a wall!'

Nurse Ryan held up a jar containing 100 Gall Stones and asked me if I wanted to take them home. Needless to say after all the pain, I didn't need a reminder!

What a fantastic Hospital that was. Every patient's mattress was turned daily by those dedicated Nurses and the standard of hygiene was superb. The food served to patients was prepared and cooked in the kitchens of the Hospital. Those days the Hospitals in Ireland were run by Nuns, and the patient's welfare was paramount. The nursing staff had remarkable bedside manners!

Emergency Services were provided by the Jubilee Nurses, who were on duty in a building at the end of Beau Street.

Beau Street I remember so well, as I had a room when I was first married in a house in the middle of Beau Street, No: 15, owned at that time by Mrs Phelan. Today it is 'The Samaritans of Waterford'.

The Fish Market in Peter's Street was very busy on Fridays. Fish Mongers, each with their own separate tables arranged along the pavements. I often bought the heads of Cod fish for a few pence in the 40's.

After washing in salted water, I simmered them in a saucepan for a few minutes on the coal fire. When cool I removed the fish from the jaws and discarded the bones.

To the fish pieces I added an onion, and cooked them gently together in milk, with a little margarine and thickened with flour. This made a very nourishing and enjoyable meal on Friday's, served with mashed potatoes. It was a great favourite with the children. The soup made from the sheep's head (purchased from Molloy's Butchers) was also delicious. The liquid, thickened with pearl barley made good soup, only the bones were thrown away. So many recipes were created from so little.

Another place I remember on my trips back home, on holidays from Coventry in the 50's is the 'Saratoga Pub' in Woodstown. When friends arranged nights out, we all gathered together in this old fashioned building, furnished with wooden benches and tables. The bar with its old counter was littered with pint sized glasses and ashtrays. As you entered, the strong smell of beer and cigarette smoke almost overwhelmed you. The atmosphere was very lively with all the singing. A lad usually provided the music by playing a melodeon box, or perhaps a piano accordion.

As the evening went on some of the men retreated to a back room for a card game, leaving the women to chat and enjoy a drink amongst themselves.

At closing time, especially at weekends, there was a dance on the roadside outside the pub, with the sounds of the sea in the distance.

Everyone by this time was quite merry and noisy with lots of quips and laughter, but no trouble. Many cars travelled back to Waterford through a very narrow and bendy roadside, often miraculously arriving safely home.

CHAPTER FIVE

October, 2008 I am planning a holiday in Ireland; it has been 5 years since my return to Coventry. I will spend some time in the Commeragh Mountains and see Billy's house for the first time. So I am looking forward to that and hope the weather will be kind to me. I will also visit my cousins in Waterford and Tramore and hope to see all my friends.

On the 7th October, 2008 Bill and Mags drove me to Birmingham for my direct flight to Waterford. We had an unusual coincidence there, as we were checking in my luggage.

A girl standing beside me said, 'Is it Brigid?'

I was taken by surprise as I did not recognise her face! Mags interrupted saying, 'Mum its Rena?'

It was in fact a Waterford girl that had stayed with us in Cheylesmore when she first arrived with my sister to find work in Coventry. It was lovely to see her after all those years and amazingly she recognised me! So we had lots to talk about as we travelled together on the Waterford flight. Sadly she was going home to attend her sister's funeral.

Kathy my daughter-in-law and cousins were at Waterford Airport waiting for me, and so my planned month's holiday began. Daylight was fading as Kathy drove through the narrow mountain Roads. We eventually reached the house, the dog barking noisily to announce our arrival.

I was a bit overcome on entering the house, seeing how much Billy had achieved in 2 years. It was a 4 bed roomed bungalow; very large entrance hall, a massive kitchen, and some of the furniture, like the dresser and bookcase he had built himself. There were solid oak floors in every room, beautifully designed ceilings, conservatory, with a view of the mountains through every window surrounding the house. Kathy designed the interior, which was really lovely, and I liked her choice of furnishings.

Amazing to think he had built this lovely house alone. There are 4 acres of land surrounding it; he will eventually have to get a couple of sheep to keep the grass trimmed. The fields adjoining the house had herds of cattle grazing peacefully.

On a clear day I could see the sea in the distance, although mist could descend quite quickly to obscure the view of the mountains. It was a very peaceful week Kathy took a day off work to take me to Dungarvan, where we 'shopped 'til we dropped.'

Weather-wise, I was lucky to get 4 good days out of 7 and with the aid of my stick; I managed to have a walk on a few mornings. On the 3 days that it rained, I busied myself baking soda bread and bread and butter pudding, this was Kathy's favourite. I enjoyed all the freshly cooked meals that were prepared for me in the evenings.

My next stay was with my cousins in Tramore, where a gathering of all my relations and a welcome home party awaited me. Some of them had travelled from Dublin, Wexford, and the nearby seaside resort of Dunmore East. I was made very welcome and comfortable in their home.

In the week that followed, it was lovely to walk around Tramore, especially the Donraile coastline, and meet my old neighbour Joan, from St Leger Villas. It was nice to see her again and she was very complimentary about my Books. I visited

Maura and Johnny and Maura's sister Bridie. We had so much to talk about.

Ann O'Connor invited me to dinner; it was a very enjoyable meal. Sister Carmel visited me at the house. We had a lovely hour together despite her busy schedule.

It was a pleasure to meet Maureen in the ever popular Cahill's Shop; she again made very kind remarks regarding my Books, especially 'The Five Children....'

I was privileged to be close to the Church, enabling me to attend 10'oclock Mass most mornings; it was great to see it so well attended. I also had the opportunity to join the Charismatic Prayer Meeting, which faithfully continues every Tuesday evening.

My cousins treated me to a lovely meal at The Pine Rooms in Tramore.

I enjoyed walking the beach again, but I must admit, the hills seemed to get steeper, and I relied very much on my walking stick.

My next week was with cousins Paul and Clair in Viewmount, Waterford, where I was also made very comfortable. As they were both retired, they looked forward to taking me sight-seeing. Paul parked on the Quay near the clock for the 'Heritage' visit, which housed the history of Waterford past and present in the Granary, also known as the Museum. The girl at Reception was pleasant and helpful. On the Tour we met a few 'Yanks' eager to share a comment or two. Before leaving we had lunch in their lovely Restaurant.

A day or so later, the next tour was by car to Waterford Castle Hotel and Golf Club on the Island. This was described so accurately in their booklet, as being fashioned by nature. It was very picturesque and enchanting. We drove onto the Ferry (which is in constant use taking visitors to and from the Island). It was quite a short journey, and we were accompanied by many golfers and tourists.

On arrival we were allowed entrance to the magnificent dining room. Waterford Crystal chandeliers hung from the ornate ceilings and the tables were beautifully laid once again with the finest of Waterford Crystal and Wedgwood China, all this with the oak panelled walls was very impressive.

The Golf course surrounding the Castle was an attraction for many professional golfers touring the Waterford area.

Tradition tells us that a Monastic settlement existed on the Island sometime between the 6th and 8th centuries! A winged angel from the 8th century and the crude carving of a Monk's head is now prominently displayed over the main entrance to the Castle, dating from the 6th century. This is just a glimpse of the history of Waterford Castle.

After a very interesting day we took the return Ferry back to the City, after having a memorable experience. Paul was so pleased that I enjoyed the day.

Our next outing was to Inistioge in Kilkenny. A film was made there, of the book 'Circle of Friends' by the famous Author Maeve Binchey. There is now, also a popular Restaurant in the village called 'Circle of Friends' where we had a lovely home cooked lunch.

We then travelled onto Tibget Estate Mansion, which was burned down during the 'Troubles.' Now only half of the walls remain. In the beautiful grounds surrounding it, there are over 20 Monkey Puzzle trees and that is unusual. To appreciate this scenery you really have to see it.

On the return journey, we passed through Graigenamanagh, where there is an historical Abbey, known as Village of the Monks. It was very interesting to walk around the Abbey and we lit candles there before leaving.

Looking back now that was a very special week.

My final week was spent with more of my cousins in Springfield, Lower Waterford. That was a fun week, again the hospitality was great.

I enjoyed the walks around the city of my childhood, now of course much updated and modern. A lot of the old buildings gone, tragic to hear the famous glass factory under threat of closure due to the worldwide recession. Let's hope it will be short lived.

My holiday came to a close with another get-together and a night out at their newest Thai Restaurant in the city.

My final visit was to my granddaughter Breige, John and the children, who also live in Waterford. We had fun looking through old photograph albums. The children Jordan, Anna and Jude, were all excited telling me about their schools, hobbies and interests.

My great-grandson Jordan is a cast member for the 'Hound' Productions and he delighted in telling me of his acting, mainly with Red Kettle Theatre Company. He drew my attention to a write-up in the 'Hound' Magazine, where he was quoted as saying, 'Well! My name is Jordan O'Regan. I'm 11 years old and attend 6th class at St. Stephen's School. I have been acting since the day I was born! Nah, not really, since I was 8 (mainly with Red Kettle). Doing 'Hound' has been deadly, just DEADLY!! Enjoy the show!!'

He sings with Waterford Boys Singers, and loves playing Rugby, his position is Scrum Half. Jordan goes on to Water Park Secondary School in September.

Anna enjoys annoying everyone at the moment and is a bit of a drama queen, but hastens to inform me that she loves disco dancing, and attends The Mercy Convent School.

Jude interrupts, telling me he plays basketball and attends St. Stephen's Delasalle School.

All three are Karate enthusiasts. They are delightful children and so well behaved.

Breige is a very caring person and works with children with Special Needs. This she finds very rewarding and the hours fit in well with the family lifestyle; which has changed so much since I was a girl in the mid thirties.

Being aged about 9, after spending the afternoon at my grandmother's house, I nearly always got a penny, leaving for home. I would look at that penny and realize it would be useful for the gas when I arrived home.

But the temptation when passing Mullins's Chip Shop on Ballybricken, was too much for me to resist. I could buy a penny worth of chips or 2 scallops, the batter on the scallops was crispy, and it crackled when I got my teeth into it. And the sharp taste of vinegar mingled with salt was delicious. I remember the taste even now. I was left with greasy hands which I mopped up with the newspaper wrappings, in case Dad or Mam smelt the chips from my hands.

It would annoy them to think that I had spent a penny that was needed for the gas. Now that might sound harsh, and yes, it was I suppose, but it instilled in me a sense of responsibility that stood to me in later years in preparation for the long hard road that lay ahead! I believe there is a reason for everything that happens to us. I did take big chances in life and also experienced the terrific urge to go ahead. Like in 1956 leaving home with my children to start a new life in England, of course I had doubts and was afraid, but what I can only describe as common sense took over. I was driven to go ahead. I'm not saying it was easy,

one step doesn't get you very far; you've got to keep on walking.

A few words from Val Doonican's song another Waterford man;

'Walk tall, walk straight and look the world right in the eye.....'

That about sums it all up, it does surprise me now though, looking back, because by nature I am very sensitive and inclined to hug my troubles, however reaching this stage of my life only my very own can hurt me. Still, I am easily embarrassed, and a worrier. I am left in no doubt that my faith saw me through all the impossible times of the 50's and 60's.

It was enlightening talking to my great-grandchildren and remembering the words of Father Guiry at my marriage service 'May you see your children's, children's children.' And amazingly I have!

I was so thankful to remain well enough to enjoy my holiday. I signed books at the Book Centre, where I was greeted by a member of staff who made me comfortable, seating me at a table and presenting me with a complimentary cup of coffee.

I visited the Museum Library, and while I was there I actually saw a lady buy my second book 'River Factory Tales,' which was a nice coincidence.

I did almost everything I wanted to do and enjoyed reflecting on all I had achieved in a month. My son, his wife and my relatives really made my stay memorable and enjoyable.

My flight back to Coventry was pleasant; I now look forward to the Christmas Season. Our unusually cold and snowy weather was unexpected. Being sheltered in the Midlands, we escaped the heavy snow drifts.

Our courtyard here in Bonds is very picturesque indeed, reminding me of winters long past.

I thank the Lord as I reflect on all the Christmas's gone by. The very simple poor ones were still joyous and magical, with soft snowflakes falling. Shops displaying lights in their windows where Santa sat, with his long white beard and beaming smile, to delight children as they passed and waved to him. Hoping he would notice them and read their thoughts on his visits on Christmas Eve night, as they imagined him coming down the chimney with their gifts while they lay sleeping!

It was all centred on the birth of Jesus, that one special baby that had come to save the world! I remember the crib padded with straw and this beautiful little baby always seemed alive to me, with Mary and Joseph protecting him.

As a young child I recalled thinking, I wish I could cover him up with a little blanket, to warm him against the bitter cold night.

Although 83 years have rolled by I'm sure children's imagination remains the same today, as they gaze at the Nativity scene; not quite understanding the mystery of Jesus, being born to a virgin in a stable, who was to be our Saviour!

Isn't it amazing that Christmas has never lost its magic. It's still Holy Night. Unfortunately by and large it has lost its true meaning. We get carried away with the excitement of eat, drink and be merry, also the exchanging of gifts. Yet the beautiful carol singing, often moving us to tears, reminds us we are celebrating the birth of Christ! It comes natural to us to remember the homeless, the elderly, the lonely, and all those less fortunate than ourselves.

It's wonderful what Christmas has instilled in us. We look forward to it each year, as we plan ahead, filled with good intentions, even though we don't always fulfil them. In our humanity we often fail.

CHAPTER SIX

Are We Facing Hard Times Again?

Recession is now upon us. The present economic crisis gives us an opportunity to stop and think, and ask ourselves what kind of society we want to live in. The present crisis marks the end of selfishness and greed. I'm sure we did lose our way a bit. Are we bringing up our children with the kind of values we want? We now have a me, me attitude. With our virtues and values diminished. I read where the Church of England voiced their opinions on the present crisis.

The Archbishop of York, John Sentamu criticized society's idolatrous love of money, while the Bishop of London, Richard Chartres pointed out that the financial crisis contained opportunities as well as suffering.

'In times of recession, people have to rely on friends, neighbours and families, the things that really matter to them, that may be a good thing.'

'A change is necessary, so that our society reflects the values of fairness and justice, and that the voices of the worst affected are heard.'

Cardinal Murphy O'Connor has given his full backing to an initiative that seeks to use Church buildings and land for affordable housing. He says, 'I am delighted to commend this initiative to all Faith communities, who are seeking to respond to the needs of the homeless or poorly housed, in evidence of hardship, which can lead to the loss of human dignity and shelter.'

These are worrying times for people who have lost their jobs and those on the verge of losing theirs. Nobody knows when this crisis will end. Perhaps we may all be better off for it! There was so much money floating around, it seemed to go to peoples heads and even with all the luxury of big fancy houses, expensive holidays abroad, and still people were not content. Everything was taken for granted.

Now we will have to 'cut the cloth to our measure.' We can't be worse off than our parents and grandparents, who really saw hard times, and every penny had to be counted but they still managed to make ends meet.

They never went out for meals, and certainly didn't know what it was to have a foreign holiday. They lived simply and were happy to be alive. So now we will have to save for what we want. We all know that anything got easy, is not worth having. No doubt we will survive, and spare a thought for people all over the world, dying from sickness and disease. I'm sure those people would love to be in our situation. Your health is your wealth!

Compassion is such an important trait in a person. You sense it very quickly. It's never lost, the eyes and attitude betray it immediately, the sense of touch like the reassuring hand on your arm that says 'I understand.'

It's almost impossible to explain the comfort it imparts to the individual, who perhaps is feeling very low and depressed, yet trying hard to conceal it.

When you live alone and your family are long gone, with responsibilities and families of their own, one must take a step back and realize this is all part of the process as we go into old age.

Still, the family play a huge part in support. It really doesn't take a lot, a phone call, a regular visit, consistency is important, and not to treat it as a duty. I feel there is no doubt the family bond is weakening, and that is very sad and serious. As I recall the old saying, 'If there is not peace in the family, how can there be peace in the world!'

Living in Sheltered accommodation, I chat often with the ladies here. It's common to hear them express, 'I hope I never become a burden' and I echo that.

In my prayers, I ask the Lord to help me not to turn into a complaining, self pitying old lady, draining my family. I feel that would be the worst thing that could happen to me. Then I would lose my dignity.

Working as a Home Help in Coventry in the 60's was a great learning experience for me. One particular lady I visited, was very trying, and opening her door with a key to let myself in, I usually greeted her with a, 'Good morning Mary. How are you today?'

The reply was always the same, 'Well how do you think I am? Here on my own, I haven't slept all night!'

Humouring her I usually said, 'Well never mind, I'm here now,' as I went about lighting her fire and preparing her breakfast, while engaging her in conversation. I had to forget my own problems, which were many to say the least.

Although she was a pain, I did feel sorry for her, as it was a cry for help. I hope I was of some comfort to that lady, I do believe I was, and I thank God for that, because he had given me the gift of compassion.

My own parents, at different times, expressed being lonely. Mammy, on one of my visits in 1971, aged 67 her health was failing, and as I helped her to make her bed, she said, 'I feel so lonely sometimes!'

Another time I travelled home on a surprise visit to Daddy, who was aged 82years and blind. I let myself in with my key and opened the kitchen door. The radio was playing and he was sitting at the table having his meal. It was a cold room; the fire glimmered in the old marble fireplace.

As I entered he turned to me and said, 'Who is it?'

Laying my hand on his shoulder, I replied, 'Its Brigid, Daddy.'

He turned and looking up at me, his sightless eyes filled with tears, he said, 'I'm alright love, but it's the loneliness that gets to me!'

This still haunts me!

We were a family of 14 children; some now deceased, others living in Britain. This meant my parents had to live out their old age in loneliness.

It's so easy to be wise in hindsight. Circumstances were such, that as teenagers we had to leave home to find work, as did many Irish families in the 40's, 50's and 60's.

These were very difficult times for families who had emigrated, to keep in touch with each other. In an ideal situation maybe, had we communicated more and taken it in turns to visit, our parents would never have felt this loneliness and isolation.

It's so easy to make excuses for neglect, and remorse is a dreadful thing. Looking around me, I'm sure it still goes on. We know our own children very well, but a day will come when even they will surprise us.

Despite that, there are some wonderful families here where I live, including my own. They take their parents out for weekends, on holidays, and out for meals. It's heartening to see such love and care still around.

Writing my books was a wonderful opportunity to express my feelings, as this is something I find very hard to do.

Being oversensitive has handicapped me all my life. I fought and tried so hard to hide the fact that I had very low self esteem, common in people with depression. This condition is very difficult to cope with, especially when one longs to portray confidence and prove they can cope. Obviously I am a strong character, although I was not aware of this trait in myself. Other people often remarked on it. As individuals we are all unique.

I admire the qualilties I see in people around me. For instance, those who look after handicapped children and the Elderly like Carers, Nurses, and Volunteers in our Hospitals. The people who visit the sick and the dying, our Missionary Nuns and Priests, who work tirelessly; also the parishioners in our Churches that clean, and take care of the Altar and flower arranging, also those that sell tickets for Church Funds and various Charities.

They must often feel embarrassed doing this, but they do it and are so consistent. I could go on and on, so much good around us all the time. But, you know the saying where there is good, evil is never far away!

Visiting the Irish Centre today in Hill Street, Coventry I was very surprised when Mary one of the Volunteers greeted me with a, 'Hello lovely lady.' She said, 'My neighbour loves your books.'

She was thrilled when I signed a Bookmark for her. She thanked me and embraced me warmly. Mary never knew that she actually made my day!

The little things we say and do can make such a difference, as we pass people in the street sometimes and often wonder what kind of problems they are hiding behind a smile.

Sometimes the very sad times in our lives, are a ticket to happiness. We think of our failures, but they never really are failures. We learn so much from them. Believe in yourself. We are called to be life givers. Life is a gift to be enjoyed. When you were born, you cried and the world rejoiced. Live and love in such a way that when you die, the world will cry and you will rejoice!

There was a story I read years ago that is as applicable even of life as it is today:

The telephone rang in this house; it was answered by a tiny voice. Which was obviously that of a child?

'Hello, is your father there?'

'No I'm sorry, he's busy.'

'Well can I speak to your mother?'

'No came the whisper, I'm sorry she's busy.'

'Is there anyone else I can talk to? Is there anyone else there?'

'There's the Fire brigade; the Ambulance and the Police' was the whispered reply.

'Can I speak to one of the men from the Fire brigade?'

'No I'm sorry they're busy.'

'Well can I speak to the driver of the Ambulance?' Asked the man, with heightened voice and impatient tone.

'No' came the whispered reply, 'He's busy.'

'Well then' asked our friend running out of patience and getting more agitated.

'Can I speak to one of the Policemen?'

'No' came the reply, 'they're busy.'

'What's happening there? Roared our friend, 'what are they all doing there?'

'They're looking for me!'

That story impressed me so much that I wrote it down, because that's how it must look to Jesus looking on, as people are running in all directions. Looking for something that is right there within their own hearts, should they choose to stop long enough and look.

Help me to be still and know that you are God.

There's a vast difference in being helpless and being hopeless.

Life can be difficult and there are times when it's not easy to retain hope and be optimistic.

We are all only human, it's so normal to have good and bad days. Worry can well be defined as not having enough faith in God!

One evening I was in a discussion Group where one man described himself as being 'all over the place' and felt he badly needed to get himself together.

This is a good example of 'the lost child!'

CHAPTER SEVEN

Lost In The Foggy Days

Many tragedies came my way during my life, I have experienced almost everything. Maybe even a little more than my fair share. The passing of time helped to diminish and ease the pain somewhat, except for the depression from which there was no escape. I had days when, I would be so delighted, everything seemed brighter and I felt like shouting,

'Thank you Lord, I feel so well today!'

Listening to my music, I sang along with my favourite songs, enjoyed my house work, and got down to my writing, while appreciating everything around me; the blue skies, the birds nesting and singing in the trees that I am lucky enough now to have outside my apartment window. I welcomed the patter of rain on the pavements, which made the air smell fresh. So much to appreciate!

I could, if only briefly, experience great peace of mind. That peace that is only God given, and just when I thought that horrible black cloud had passed, back the depression would come and often with a vengeance. No explaining it and so very hard to describe to anyone. Who would want to know anyway? When you were asked how you were, you replied, 'I'm fine thank you, how are you?' But really, wanting to scream and perhaps say, 'I feel there is nothing to live for anymore.'

Is depression hereditary?

I believe some forms are. My father had a drink problem, later in life I wondered was the real problem clinical depression. As a young child, I noticed he was mostly very sad and cried easily, when he was drunk. In the mornings his hands would tremble as he poured our tea.

As the years rolled on, it was obvious how inadequate daddy really was, and when he did find work. Mammy was never sure whether he would bring the wages home or not. So that was an impossible situation for her.

In later years I realized how torn I was with the circumstances at home, and pride stood in the way of me being able to confide in anyone!

Marrying young, I went from the frying pan into the fire! And at the age of 38 I suffered a nervous breakdown. I was hospitalized at Louise Raines, a building situated close to the Central Hospital in Warwick. It was a very frightening experience.

Several procedures began; the first was long talks with the Psychiatrist. Sitting there not feeling very much emot-

ion, even beyond being nervous, the thought crossed my mind; this man must be very clever if he can help me. I mean, I can't even understand myself. I heard him say his name as he introduced himself and shook hands with me, asking, 'How do you feel today?'

Lost for words to describe my state of mind, replying I said,' I can't describe it, I just feel numb!'

He went back to my childhood, asking 'What my relationship was like with my parents?' 'Did I feel loved?' 'What my schooling was like?' 'Did I excel in any subjects?' Was it difficult for me to learn and concentrate? And so he continued to make notes on my background. I answered as well and as truthfully as I could.

It was the early 60's; medication was widely used, as well as E.C.T. and Pentethol (known then as the 'Truth Drug.') The side effects were horrific, especially after the 'Shock Treatment,' I was vomiting, couldn't remember my name, not that it mattered much. The Pentethol was an escape for me. After the injection, I drifted into oblivion, as a Doctor sat with me.

On awakening, slowly opening my eyes, my first thought was, 'Oh please God, I'm not back!'

I focused on the nurse, who was sitting beside me as she held my hand. She was smiling. I envied her being able to smile; I was then 39 years old.

My eldest child was 17 and the youngest 8 years – lovely children, and I wasn't there for them! What had happened to me? I tried to concentrate on their names, and imagine their faces, but it wouldn't penetrate my mind. I wished I could go to sleep, but sleep wouldn't come without medication. I longed for bedtime when I would get my sleeping tablet. A large capsule, coloured red and blue, it was called 'Tuinel.' It was quick acting, and wonderful to feel myself drifting off to sleep, but wide awake early to start yet another long day of confusion and isolation.

After washing and dressing which was a big effort, then going to the dining hall for breakfast, and back to the Ward. Nurses were floating about arranging to take us for walks in groups, or maybe Occupational Therapy, perhaps sitting in a room listening to music and encouraging patients to dance to the rhythm of the music.

Some patients may even dance, others would just sit, deep in thought, fiddling with a handkerchief, or some other object, others searching endlessly in their handbags, that were usually very cluttered. Or there could be patients weepy, and following a nurse around, asking questions that didn't make sense, being comforted by the nurse, or assistant and led back to their chairs. There were different age groups, ranging from 16 to 65years.

The medicine trolley was pushed around three times a day, by senior staff. Patients were lined up to be given their prescribed dose of medication, and watched closely to ensure they swallowed their tablets, when given a glass of water.

Some confused patients were likely to drop the tablets into their pockets, or handbags, deciding to take them later. It was common for nurses to find tablets hidden under pillows at night.

For the E.C.T. Treatment days, we lined up, sitting on a bench, as we were taken one-by-one into the treatment room; where several beds were neatly made up with sheets folded back, and equipment fitted to the end of each bed, for Electric Shock Treatment.

Straps were fastened across the patient's chest and legs, and then an injection was given to prevent remembering anything afterwards.

The beds were then pushed into the Recovery room. Eventually the patient woke up, very dazed with a severe headache and feeling sick. A receiver was placed near their shoulder. Vomiting was distressing and weakening. Patients were affected in different ways; one young woman I got to know, had an obsession about hell, and eventually had a Leucotomy operation, which sounded drastic to me!

I lost touch with her, so I never knew the outcome, though she often crossed my mind.

I wasn't responding to E.C.T. and it was difficult to find the medication I could tolerate. One drug I remember was 'Concordion;' this gave me breathing problems and confusion. It was 10mg, and considered a low dose.

When I was eventually stabilised on suitable medication, I was allowed home for weekends only. Washing was piled up, waiting to be done, the house was disorganised, the children were coping the best way they could, and delighted to have me home again.

I was discharged after 9 weeks, but still not coping with my affairs. The Psychiatrists had a long talk with me, telling me that my recovery would be slow, and indeed it was! I had a Social Worker calling for several weeks; I also attended relaxation classes in Coventry and Warwick Hospital every week for 3 months.

Self pity is a big factor in depression. The self pitier feels they have no rights, allowing people to use and manipulate them. Take advantage of them, so they end up licking their wounds.

Crying in privacy and suffering silently, often feeling they have no right to stand up for themselves, with very unhealthy consequences. They almost become a doormat, developing a fear of being selfish and self centred, and for some unknown reason feeling they must always be wrong. Not realising some selfishness is perfectly sane and healthy. The word selfish is misleading, and not a nice word, as it suggests wanting ones own way completely. That is a childish way to live and not worth mentioning, but change it around a bit and call it enlightenment.

Have you ever noticed the strong people in your life? They don't let themselves be pushed around; they don't feel sorry for themselves. When hurt or injured, they immediately become assertive. There lies the key in protecting yourself from becoming a doormat. To avoid this trap, remember no one controls you without you allowing it.

Now all this is easier said than done, especially when you are clawing your way out of depression, but with time, patience and determination you can come through it. Because when you reach the bottom there is only one way you can go, and that is up.

Today 2008, Psychiatry has moved forward so much, you will not be prescribed some medications so easily. There are Social Workers, Psychologists, and Group Therapy; still it is in my own opinion an illness that is greatly misunderstood.

Having often being physically ill, (like having a hysterectomy, and indeed a few operations) at least something could be done! Even a heart attack, which was very frightening, I overcame in time.

Being anxious certainly delayed recovery, but eventually I survived all these setbacks. Yet the depression always managed to get to me.

I coped with it by telling myself, 'It won't last, it will pass.'

Working through the bad days, keeping myself busy, I may start decorating, and would often cry as I was stripping walls of the old paper, and gathering it in to bin bags. Perhaps I would go for a walk, or play music. Ironically as I write this, there is a Doctor being interviewed on T.V. The discussion is 'Mental Illness.' Now so wide spread, especially in children. It's aggravated by binge drinking, broken homes, anxiety and drug taking!

The biggest problem now it appears is lack of Specialist treatment. Maybe again the root of the problem is depression, leading them to drown their sorrows (so to speak), as they seek consolation in socializing and losing themselves in alcohol, and so they go on. Myself I don't like the taste of alcohol, so maybe, but for the grace of God, there go I!

My own experience was that if you tried to explain how you felt, it was dismissed with a wave of the hand. 'It's your imagination' 'or' 'pull yourself together!' Consequently you went into yourself. Fortunately l was a strong character and managed to cope.

If you had a broken wrist and your hand was in a sling, it was obvious, and people would offer to help. But with depression, they just can't understand what the problem is. And you don't understand it yourself, so it's very difficult for everyone.

I had a very busy life so I struggled on, but of course it did eventually catch up with me, with a vengeance.

I read somewhere that Winston Churchill called his depression, 'the black dog' that followed him!

It's very important to have an understanding of what's happening to you and seek professional help early. I was sensitive as to what people thought of me – a big mistake! I did find the clergy helpful; they have a great insight into anything emotional. It's all part of their training.

I prayed when I was able, I do believe it helped me a lot. Some people get 'the blues' or 'that fed up feeling' so might casually remark, 'I feel like that sometimes.' But they are so far from depression, it's not true.

So my advice, as someone who has experienced severe depression and a 'breakdown.' Seek help early from trained people. It's a long journey but the 'black cloud' will pass, and you will often emerge a stronger person.

It is believed that 1 in 5 people will suffer with depression at some time in their lives! But it has to be dealt with. It has a huge effect on close ones.

Compassion is very important, but at the same time keeping a distance, in case one gets bogged down. To keep a diary is a good idea, making a note of how you feel from day to day.

Get information – don't stay in a small space. Pick up the phone, talk to a friend and don't let it be a life sentence! It's very difficult because you do feel above all; you don't want to drag people down with you.

Depression is a double burden when you are a parent. With the added darkness in your children's lives; they must struggle to cope, and the parent has to maintain the role of guarding their children's future.

The depression is mystifying, not only to the sufferer but also those around them. It profoundly affects relationships. Parents also feel guilty and often ashamed of having the illness, and tend to isolate themselves with their fears. Confusion about depression prevents families seeking help with the problem; they often feel prejudice from outside, with the stigma attached to mental illness. Depression is just as much a medical problem as heart disease or diabetes and is highly treatable.

I found Psychiatry very helpful. The after care and counselling was excellent.

Thankfully today, with all the research that has been done in Psychiatry, patients with depression can choose the kind of treatment they want. Some may well prefer medication. Some may decide on talking therapies, while others a combination of both.

I like meditation, it's difficult to begin with, but if you are serious about meditation, you have to persevere on a daily basis.

Silence is the best preparation for meditation. When you begin to meditate, spend a couple of moments getting really comfortable.

If you want to sit in a chair, sit in an up-right one. If you sit on the floor, sit in a comfortable position. Then try to be as still as you can for the entire time of the meditation.

When you are seated and are still, close your eyes and then begin to repeat, silently in your heart, the word 'Maranatha.'

In some traditions this is called Mantra, a 'prayer phrase or prayer word.'

The essence of meditation as explained by John Main OSB., in his book 'The Path of Meditation, 'is simply learning to say that word. To recite it, from the beginning to the end of the meditation - It is utterly simple. Say it like this: 'Ma-ra-na-tha.' Four equally stressed syllables.

The speed is something that is fairly slow, fairly rhythm-

ical, 'Ma-ra-na-tha,' and that is all you need to know in order to meditate.

Religion also plays a big part in the recovery from depression. It gives the patient hope and something to hold on to in the difficult days.

This is a subject I feel very passionate about. At this advanced age, I understand depression a lot better, thanks to my GP and Psychiatry; I am still here to tell my story!

It is a difficult subject to write about and impossible to explain symptoms, as we all describe our feelings differently. But I feel it is very important to be more open and sympathetic about depression, in our attitudes.

These days there doesn't seem to be enough time to sit and listen. Then of course this does take a certain type of person. I hope my experience will help someone along that lonely, uphill road, so hard to climb!

CHAPTER EIGHT

The following write-ups are from a book of one of my favourite Authors, Father Jack McArdle. Not too heavy but very interesting.

Hope and Despair

There were two boys one time, and one was a pessimist, the other was an optimist.

One would find something wrong in heaven; he could never appreciate what he had, because he was always conscious of what he did not have.

The optimist was full of hope, and, even if his team was beaten by ten goals, he was quite hopeful they would win next time out. Anyhow, the pessimist was put into a room full of toys, and the optimist was put in a room filled with manure from the farmyard.

After an hour, they were checked on. The pessimist was sitting in the middle of all the toys and he was crying. When asked why he was crying, he replied that he was crying because there was no drum!

When the door of the optimist's room was opened, he wasn't aware of that, because he was really busy with a small shovel, and he was shovelling the manure from one corner of the room to the other.

He was interrupted, and asked what he was doing; he replied, his eyes filled with excitement. 'With all this manure, there's got to be a pony here somewhere!'

And that, my friends, is the difference between hope and despair.

Of course, we have to struggle, to shovel, and to work hard, but Jesus guarantees the results. That is an extraordinary aspect of the Christian faith. As I attend a funeral, and see the tears of genuine anguish, I would be present at a school for despair if that was the end of it all.

However, as Christians, we believe that it's certainly not the end, and the very best is yet to come.

Where We Leave Our Clothes

A man was strolling through a Cemetery with his little 4 year old daughter. She pointed to the tomb stones and asked him what they are for. He was really puzzled how best to explain something like this to a 4 year old.

'These were people who lived in those houses down there, and then, one day, God asked them to come and live with him in his house!'

There was a moment's silence, and then another question.

'And daddy, did they go off to live in holy God's house?'

'Yes.' said the father, hoping to end the discussion.

Then the little girl's eyes lit up, as she looked up at her dad and said, 'And guess what daddy, I bet you when they went off to live in holy God's house this is where they left their clothes!'

And, you know something, she was spot-on. This is where they left their clothes, which they don't need now.

I will never go into a coffin. The body I now live in will probably end up in a coffin, but, by then, I will have gone ahead, to become what I was created to be. It is after I pass through the second birth, which we call death, that I will become what God created me to be.

The Lily Pond

There were grubs crawling around in the bottom of a pond. They were talking, and wondering whatever happens to those among them who have crawled up the stem on top, and never returned. They wondered what it would be like up there. They made an agreement with each other that the next grub to climb the stems of the lilies would return to tell the others what it was like up there. Sure enough, after some time, one felt drawn to the surface. He climbed to the top and out on a leaf on the lily pond. It was so bright here, so bright and so warm. It had been so dark and cold down below. Suddenly, something started to happen to him, as he began to change, to open out, to discover that he had two beautiful wings, he had actually become a beautiful dragon-fly, which he was created to be in the first place.

He had no idea of this, as he thought he was supposed to remain a grub, or a caterpillar, all his life. He flew back and forth across the pond. He could see them below, but they could not see him. There was no way he could get back to them. After a while, he gave up trying, because, he concluded, 'Even if they could see me, they would never believe that a beautiful creature like me was ever one of them.'

There is a very wide gap between one stage of life and the next.

The Twin Babies

Imagine if the unborn baby could think, it would be terrified of dying, because it is moving out of the only world it knows.

Once there were twin boys in their mother's womb. After some time, they became aware of the cord. And after further discussion and examination, they decided that their mother must really love them, because she was sharing her very life with them.

Sometime further on, they became aware of changes occurring in themselves. They noticed tiny nails appearing on their fingers; they noticed little eye-brows, eye lashes etc. They wondered what this could mean. Then one of them suggested that they were maybe getting ready to be born. The other little guy cringed, 'I don't want to be born. I want to stay where I am.'

'But we have to be born,' said the other little guy. 'We cannot stay here all our lives.'

'How do you know there's any life after this? Have you ever seen anyone that was born? Did any of them ever come back to tell us what it's like? There just has to be life after this. If this is it, it makes no sense at all. I honestly believe that we are here preparing for the next stage, whatever that will be.'

'But how do you know there's a mother? What does she look like? Have you ever seen her? I bet you we only invented her for our own security.'

And so, the argument went back and forth.

One was already a little atheist, while the other was a man of faith, which, in simple English, meant that he believed something, but had proof for nothing!

And finally the time came, and they were born.

When it was safe to do so, they opened their eyes, and found themselves looking up into the face of their mother.

They looked at each other, as if to say, Weren't we very foolish. There was no way we could ever had imagined what this was going to be like. It is now obvious that we had to be born to get an idea. And so it is with us, now.

We can argue and argue till the cows come home, but we will really have to pass through the next birth, before we'll have any idea what it's all about.

We sometimes hear it said that no one comes back to tell us what it's like? I think it would be a waste of time, because it would be like the dragon-fly, and the grubs, or you and the unborn baby … the gap would be too wide, and, in the words of St. Paul, 'Eye has not seen, nor ear heard, nor has it entered into the heart of people to imagine what God has in store for those who love him.'

A Hotline to God

An elderly husband and wife were chatting, and they made a pact. When one of them died, the other would mourn for only a limited time, then collect the Insurance money, and have a really good holiday. After a while, the man said, 'Mary, do you know what I was thinking? When one of us dies, I think I'll probably go to New York.'

Notice it's always the other people who die all the time. Someday … someday … it will be my turn …

'The bell tolls for thee.'

There was a rich man one time, who heard of a priest who was reputed to have a hot line to God. The man came to him with a most unusual request. He asked the priest if he could find out for him if he would definitely go to heaven when he died. The request was unusual, but the offer was tempting, because the man offered to make a very generous contribution to a new church being built. The priest agreed to take on the task. After a while, the man returned to ask him if he had received an answer to his query. The priest said he had. When the man asked what the answer was, the priest told him that he had good news for him, and he had bad news for him, and he asked which news the man wanted to hear first. The man was taken aback somewhat, but he asked for the good news first. The priest told him that, yes, he was going to heaven when he dies. The man was delighted, and he felt that with this good news, what could possibly be bad news after that. The priest replied, 'The bad news is that you are going tonight!'

It's strange, isn't it, that the second part should be seen as bad news? Everybody wants to go to heaven, but nobody wants to die!

Father Jack McArdle (S, S.C, C.), Philosophy on life is very comforting.

CHAPTER NINE

Trash Or Treasure

Charity Shops are fascinating and many deserving charities are assisted and supported by them; The Cancer Research, the very important Myton Hospice, Children in Need, A.C.O.R.N. the Heart Foundation, The Handicapped, the animal charities like the P.D.S.A, the R.S.P.C.A., Oxfam, Extra Care, Sue Ryder, Y.M.C.A and many more.

Volunteers get great satisfaction giving their spare time in assisting them. Some of them, like students for instance, obtain experience in abundance. All these good people work so hard and unselfishly to help others, and get a lot of satisfaction from their work. Most of them I have spoken with will say, they enjoy meeting people and the work every day is different.

The excitement of opening up the huge amount of donated bags that are delivered, containing all kinds of everything, from clothes, to old items like, antiques and pictures of every description. It makes you wonder sometimes what story lies behind them. Previously they may have been hidden away in an attic somewhere, and no further use to the occupants of the house they once belonged to.

When there is a house clearance due to families emigrating; or old folks die, leaving behind many things that are precious to them, which will now be donated to their chosen charity; and often purchased by students starting up homes in bed-sits.

Dealers eagerly seeking antiques there; couples that are struggling to make ends meet will find great bargains, enabling them to get a home together.

People from the Theatre world doing shows can find suitable outfits.

Wedding clothes are another attraction and save the customer a fortune.

There is also fancy dress for themed parties.

Behind the scenes lots of recycling goes on, with articles not considered suitable for sale, such as; duvets, pillows etc.

A volunteer plays a nostalgic tape, from a Radio that perhaps had been handed in and she sings along with it.

This of course is infectious and rubs off, encouraging a customer to join in the singing. A conversation starts up discussing the tape; wondering when it was made and who sang it.

So there is entertainment surrounding you, no doubt lifting someone's spirits, who had perhaps felt quite down and suddenly was uplifted. Music is a great tonic, and often recalls pleasant memories.

People on their own and often lonely, like to visit the charity shops and just wander around, admiring the old ornaments and clothing; often picking up a bargain and chatting with the friendly ladies and gentlemen serving, exchanging the topics and news of the day.

Laughter can frequently be heard from the back of the shop, perhaps the volunteer's are trying on a hat or dress to do the catwalk?

At a guess the charity shops started off in the 1960's and grew rapidly.

It's amazing to think of the time that goes in to the sorting out of the donations. Steam cleaning the garments and arranging them on rails; ladies, men's and children's clothing; pricing and stacking the books, videos, d.v.d.'s, records, cassettes and bric-a-brac, getting shoes in order, scarves, belts and endless jewellery!

Separating winter garments from the summer items, putting them into large bags to store for the different seasons, is hard work. But nobody complains because it's such a good cause.

These charity shops are no comparison to what I remember in Ireland in the 40's. They were little shops or houses, trading in what was called 'hand me downs.' Very unattractive clothes, displayed in a small window and then perhaps sold to the Dealers, and these were resold to the public for a few pence.

I guess somebody must have bought them. Now of course the charity shops in Ireland are similar to the ones here and garments tastefully displayed.

The quality of the donated clothing is amazing. So its little wonder one overhears the remark,

'I wish they had those shops when my children were small.'

There is no excuse nowadays for anybody looking shabby or unkempt.

Driving along a Street in Coventry one day with my daughter, I noticed a very elegant lady in her wheelchair wearing a black velvet jacket with a hint of maroon in the grooved sleeves, similar to that of mink and not easily mistaken.

I remarked to Mags, 'Look, that jacket was mine,'

And this lady wore it beautifully. It made my day.

I had originally purchased it from a charity shop and had it in my wardrobe for 4 years and only wore it on special occasions such as Christmas, and it was always admired. It still drew my attention today!

Worn so confidently and casually by this lady, who obviously had excellent taste. But of course she had, after all it was my coat she chose!

When Children accompanied by their parents walk in to the shop and they see a big cuddly teddy bear or maybe a doll, their eyes light up with excitement, as they say,

'Mummy, mummy can I have this?'

The jigsaws and books are very educational for the children and can be bought for as little as 25p, 30p or 60p depending on condition. And last but not least, you can find new clothes for babies and young children, possibly unwanted gifts, still in the original wrappings.

Ruth works as a volunteer for the P.D.S.A. and she recalls vividly one day when a lady came into the shop looking for crystal wine goblets for a dinner party. Unfortunately she had broken a glass from her expensive set that morning. Showing the lady where the glasses were, she could not believe her luck when she spotted an identical glass to the one she had broken!

She left the shop one very happy lady. It just goes to show, you never know what you will find in a charity shop.

Designer clothes are frequently donated; people can look well dressed and beautifully co-ordinated for perhaps £20.

Dress £4; hat £3, shoes £3, jacket £3, bag £3, scarf £1, jewellery (assorted) £3, worn together can look gorgeous. Try it!

I never worked in a charity shop myself, being too busy when I was a young woman, making a living and rearing a family, but I do admire the people that work so tirelessly and cheerfully for this great cause.

There are people of course that find it below their dignity to frequent a charity shop, though I can admire people that do, and think how enterprising of them. After all if you purchase a new dress from even an exclusive store and wash it, it's then considered second hand, and immediately looses it's former value. So reverse the procedure, and you have a wonderful bargain and no debt!

Now that we are in a recession, hopefully charity shops will become even more popular.

CHAPTER TEN

The Golden Years

I am fascinated by antiques, and can easily slip into a nostalgic mood. Not surprising I suppose, as I have lived in 23 properties during my life, and the houses were mostly old!

In 1995 as I was moving from Waterford to Tramore, I remember asking Doctor McCann, if he would keep me on his patient list. He did give me a rather long look, as he said, 'Ok I will, as I think there is a bit of a gypsy in you, and know doubt you will be back again!'

You know something; he must have been psychic, because in 2003, I returned to live in Cathedral Square in Waterford City.

And these days as I watch the television programme 'Homes under the Hammer,' I am absolutely hypnotized in the buying and selling of the properties. I know, if I should come into money at any time during my life, I would definitely invest in a property by the sea in Ireland.

I can imagine myself advising my decorator on the décor, as I drifted from room to room, planning and arranging the gorgeous furniture. I would stand by the open window, sipping my coffee and sniffing the sea air.

Oh well, I was always a dreamer anyway, but many a true word is spoken in gest. Who knows, perhaps it may happen, and I will be spending the rest of my days travelling between Ireland and Bonds Hospital!

I would be hoping that Billy would be the Caretaker and do all the repairs. Mind you, I do say this with tongue in cheek! I can only try to imagine the expression on his face as he reads this.

The house would be my gift to my children, when I am no longer around, and hope they would remember me when spending their holidays there with their families. The house would have to be named, 'Brigid Boggan's – Journeys End.'

In the meantime I will just dream on!

Here's a song, was never sung/ growing old, is dying young!

Another programme that I like to watch, is 'Strictly Come Dancing.' It puts me in mind of 'The Olympia' in Waterford in the 40's and 50's.

The section of the ballroom with the band sitting proudly at the top, elevated on the band stand. Elegantly attired in their black ties and dinner jackets; with their drums, saxophones, trumpets and trombones.

A slow foxtrot was a very romantic dance, and the quickstep, a fun loving lively fandango.

The men wore suits, shirts and ties. With Brylcreamed, shiny hair, parted on the left side, or worn straight back.

The ladies varied in their dress. Sporting the new look skirts and sweaters, looking very glamorous, and wearing several strings of pearls, which were fashionable then. The hairstyles were usually wavy and shoulder length. The shoes were the six inch stilettos heels.

The girls nearly always arrived early for the dance. Then you had to leave your coat in, and keep your ticket safe. Making your way to the ladies room, freshen up and apply your lipstick, and check that your seams were straight in the nylon stockings.

Mostly the girls were in pairs, and reassured each other that they looked ok to emerge. Bracing yourself, you headed for the ballroom.

Sometimes we lit up a cigarette as we waited, adopting a casual manner, until the MC announced the dance; a slow waltz, foxtrot, or maybe a tango.

And the men approaching, hoping they wouldn't meet with a refusal. (Oh yes, that did happen occasionally). They might tap you on the shoulder with a 'Would you like to dance please?'

Or the more casual approach with the arm stretched out, and you glided towards him. And you both took off, often in long strides, hoping the way was clear!

He may open the conversation with, 'I don't remember seeing you here before,' or 'Do you come here often?'

There were times you thought the dance would never end, you were sure he had two left feet! Ah, but there were also the times when you wished the dance would go on forever.

The most striking thing I remember is, they danced modestly, a few inches apart. But I suppose there was always the exception, when you caught sight of the cheek-to-cheek Romeo, clutching his partner very close.

Then there was the ladies choice, usually it was just the one. I especially enjoyed the slow waltz, when the band played, 'When your hearts on fire, you must realize, smoke gets in your eyes .... '

The last dance was 'Good Night Sweetheart' and the guy asked it he could see you home. It was a walk all the way home! No cars around then, and taxis were rare and too expensive.

These were poor times, simple, romantic and happy too. What lovely memories of those wholesome days.

The following paragraph is a quotation from a great mind.

The old - like children – talk to themselves, for they have reached that hopeless wisdom of experience, which knows that though one were to cry it in the Street to multitudes, or whisper it in the kiss to one's beloved, the only ears that hear it, are one's own!

It is questionable what old age really means these days. When I was young, 35-40 was considered middle aged. I can remember women in their 50's, complaining of being so tired, and it was common to hear them say on some afternoons,

'I am going to have a lie down!'

Grandmothers and grandad lived with the family. It was almost unheard of for them to live on their own, and at that time, they didn't have big houses. It was usually '2 up and 2 down,' but they managed somehow, and fitted in very well with the household routine.

Grandma helped with chores such as; washing, cooking, and babysitting, perhaps granddad did the gardening, and was a familiar figure, sitting by the fire, often reading the paper and studying the racing pages of the day.

Those were happy families, and when the grandparents grew old and needed care, they were mostly looked after by the family.

Neighbours would visit and offer to help. A priest called on a weekly basis to visit the sick person, so Spiritual help was also provided.

There was a caring attitude in those days, I personally knew one old lady that had to be admitted to Hospital after a fall in her local Church. She was visited twice daily by her daughters and this was as recent as the late 90's in Ireland.

I remarked to one of the girls, 'Isn't she lucky to have such a caring family?'

'Well not really, she said, it's we who are lucky to still have her!'

There was no such thing as Sheltered Housing, or Care Homes in those days. It could be said this has lifted the responsibility from the families a great deal. Older people have become more independent. Sheltered accommodation does mean you have to be totally independent, and I do feel that spurs us all on to be more active. Taking part in 'Outings,' Scrabble and Line Dancing.

There are some of the ladies and gents, living here in Bonds, in their 9th decade, and still go out daily with their shopping trolleys. And when the time comes, when they can no longer look after themselves, every effort is made to find a suitable Care Home for them.

After all, we are all born to die. That's one thing we can be sure of!

My youngest son once said to me, 'Just imagine, if you had to live forever, can you think of anything worse?'

And I must admit I can't!

A good neighbour is very important, when someone says, 'I'm here if you need me.' One never feels alone with that kind of support and reassurance.

I notice people do look out for each other here. Of course, everyone likes their own space and as long as you respect that, it makes people feel comfortable and at ease.

We recently had our 500 years, Quincentenary. The service of thanksgiving was given by The Vicar, Reverend David Mayhew in Holy Trinity Church, and was very inspiring. The hymns were beautifully sung by the choir.

Following the service, we enjoyed a sit down buffet, and were entertained by a flautist and harp music. We were addressed by, Roger Bailey (A Blue Badge Guide, City Councillor, and local Historian).

He spoke of the generosity of William Ford, William Pisford and William Wigston. At a time when little support was available for those who fell on hard times. He then proposed a toast to the memory of the three Williams.

The Mayor and Mayoress of Coventry were also in attendance.

A coach was provided to take all the residents to and from the celebrations. It was a lovely occasion.

The few residents in wheelchairs were taken care of by the staff, and arriving back home to our flats, it was nice to put our feet up and read the history of 'The Alms Houses,' from the commemorative picture cards, which were placed on the buffet table for each one of us.

Now that we have reached the 'evening' of our lives, I'm sure I speak for all the residents, as I express how much we appreciate the comfortable accommodation provided for us in Bonds Hospital.

It is remarkable to see the friendship that develops between the residents here, you can spot it a mile away.

I am sure many of you have heard the following quotations, that I feel ring very true:

A friend is someone who knows all about you and still likes you.

Hold a true friend with both your hands.

The friendship that comes to an end, never really began.

We die as often as we lose a friend.

A true friend is the greatest of all blessings, and that which we take the least care to acquire.

My neighbour Angela hails from a village in Southern Ireland. She is a great story teller, and recalls having to walk 3 miles to school each day with her sisters, in the 1930's, and being taught by her mother to make soda bread, at the tender age of 9. So we have a lot in common, and enjoy each others company.

We walk to Church together, and chat about growing up during our childhood in Ireland in the lean years.

I get on with people in general. But, no doubt we can experience clashes of personality from time to time, as we are all unique. Sometimes I find myself thinking very deeply about this. It strikes me as amazing that there are not two faces or fingerprints identical in the whole world. There will be similarities of course, but always a difference.

Our sense of humour is different; usually the Irish have the ability to laugh at themselves. The English are known to be good actors. Wales is famous for their singers and we mustn't forget the canny Scots and their beautiful scenic country.

CHAPTER ELEVEN

Sunday, May 9th dawned and it was a beautiful sunny day. We left at 9.15am to make our way to St. Patricks R.C. Church, Deedmore Road, Coventry, to celebrate Mass and the Sacrament of the First Holy Communion of my great-granddaughter Katie. Her older sister Erin Rose was Confirmed in February at the same Church.

Father Paul celebrated the Mass; it was a very moving experience.

There were at least 3 rows of pews reserved for the children, as they marched in single file to take their seats, the choir sang beautifully in the background.

The boys were nicely attired in their white shirts and long trousers, and the girls' in their dresses and veils, they looked like little brides.

The Gospel of the day was:

I am the vine, you are the branches. Cut off from me, you can do nothing …

The Homily was delivered by Father Paul, a very appropriate sermon for this special day. I'm sure the children were too young to understand the meaning of the Gospel story.

But no doubt they will always carry in their hearts, the memory of their First Holy Communion, as I did mine!

I shed a tear as I watched them in procession, returning to their seats after receiving The Sacred Host, hoping their lives would be happy and fruitful.

I found myself studying the beautiful shoes worn by all of the children. I giggled and I cried at the memory of the odd black and white plimsolls, worn by my own sister Bubbles, for her First Holy Communion in Waterford, way back in the late 1930's!

Such a lot lies ahead of those little children. A mother carries and delivers a child by birth once, but by car for the next 16 years!

As we become adults we don't like control. The older we get, the more we dread losing our independence, but we must also realize we are never totally independent.

A little thought will show us how dependent we really are on many things.

After the Church ceremony, we all made our way to the Holiday Inn, Walsgrave Triangle in Coventry, where we were joined by family and friend, for a Carvery lunch.

My granddaughter Kate had returned just in time from a 3 month cruise, where she was the only medical person, along with 2 Doctors on the voyage.

She told me about all her adventures on the ship. It was a wonderful opportunity for her to travel and visit so many different countries, but however, she has decided against it as a permanent position.

We had a very interesting conversation; she will now be returning to her position as Nursing Sister at University Hospital, Coventry.

My eldest granddaughter Breige and her little girl Anna travelled from Waterford to be with us for the event. So there was a lot of news to catch up on.

At these family gatherings, we reminisce a lot. Breige reminded me of the time back in the 1980's, when Deborah and herself stayed with me at my house in Stoke.

They would leave for school together at 8.30 in the mornings, but what she remembers most of all, is when I sat at the table every Friday night, with several marked envelopes in hand, to enclose my weekly payments for;

Electricity, Insurance, Milk money, Phone, Groceries, Saturday Fund and so on.

She also recalls me setting the table at night for my son Billy's supper, with sandwiches and often cake, ready for him when he got home.

One night she asked why I kept doing that, and questioned why he couldn't do it himself.

I explained, 'Well Breige, I only do it because he makes such a mess in the kitchen, that I then have to clean up, in the morning.'

My example obviously made an impact on Breige, now she tells me that she does the same thing for her husband, for exactly the same reason!

We were interrupted by the staff announcing that our meal was ready. We made our way to the tables. It was an enjoyable lunch, and afterwards the children had a ball!

All the little cousins were getting together and running around the grounds, making the most of the day, and the lovely weather.

I had a rather deep and interesting conversation with Paul; he was very complimentary about my books. And getting back once again to the reference of the shoes, he recalled often having to use cardboard, to cover the hole in the sole of his school shoes!

'And that would only be about 38-40 years ago.'

'Now,' He said, 'my children have about 10 pairs of shoes!'

What a contrast from then and now.

As the day wore on, I was very surprised to be approached by one of my readers.

She handed me a beautiful, handwritten card, which expressed, how she had actually walked through the streets of Coventry with me, as she read my last book 'Never Had It So Good.'

A special thanks to Maureen and Nina, for your kind remarks.

A little later on Kathleen approached me, a very warm lady. Embracing me, she reminded me she had attended my first Book Launch, and hoping there will be more to come, God willing.

As we were all preparing to leave the reception, my grand -daughter Paula introduced me to a lady from Clonmel near Waterford.

This lady remembered seeing an article about my books in the paper, but as yet had not read any of them.

'Now I have met the Author,' she said, 'I will make a point of reading them.'

So it was a very eventful, enjoyable day all round.

Travelling in the car with my daughter Annie, she informed me that she had a phone call from her son Steve, in Australia. He announced his Engagement to his girl friend Emma, the day before, Saturday, 9th May. They plan to marry in 2011.

He has recently started his own business in Law and Accountancy in Australia. In spite of the recession, he is doing well.

The family are all very pleased for them both.

We have yet another First Holy Communion coming up on Saturday the 16th, for Alana, another of my great-granddaughter's.

Parents work hard for these very special occasions, but I think particularly mothers. They feel so proud, dressing the children to every last detail, and assuring them how pretty they look, and how special this day is in their lives.

I enjoyed my own children most, when they were totally dependent on me. Bathing, comforting them and watching them as they slept. Some times they smiled in their sleep.

In Ireland it was believed they saw Angels, when they smiled, and if they yawned and got hiccups, this meant they were thriving.

I always thought, if they hiccupped it was more likely the baby had indigestion!

Babies are so vulnerable, that it is even painful to think about. The concern of a mother for her baby can be very intense, even if the baby cries you feel their discomfort.

I recall a song I heard back home in Waterford, many, many years ago.

These are the words of the song.
Tired hands, that guided me through childhood days,
Tired hands, that loved and understood always,
Tired steps, that I can't number,
Tired eyes, too tired for slumber,
Tired knees, too tired for the Rosary,
But not too tired, to pray for me.
God gave her to you,
Need I tell you who,
Rocked your cradle, with those tired hands.

I think these words speak volumes in this song!

A mother holds her child's hand for a while, but their hearts forever!

Saturday, 16th May was a showery, windy day. It was a busy morning in preparation for Alana's First Holy Communion, at Christ the King R.C. Church in Coventry.

As we all live quite a distance away from each other, my lift to the Church for 12.o'clock Mass was arranged.

Alana's Nanny, Mary made her dress. It was of satin material and ankle length; the short sleeves were detailed with tiny bows, and a string of pearls were scalloped around the hemline.

She also made her wrist bag, to match the dress. It was simplicity itself.

The outfit was completed by a very fine veil, draped to her waist, together with her sequined shoes, which were a gift from her Nanny Mags.

All the children looked beautiful for their special day.

Six children said the Bidding prayers. Alana was the fourth child to read, this she did very well.

After the Gospel, Father Tom read the Homily and welcomed everyone to the Mass. He praised the parents for all their efforts in making the day so special for their children.

He thanked Deacon Gerry in preparing the children for this wonderful Sacrament, which they would remember for the rest of their lives.

The hymns were beautifully sung by the choir, and the atmosphere was reverent and very moving.

On leaving the Church, the children and parents gathered for photographs. Then we left for the reception, which was held at The Convoy, Penny Park Lane in Coventry.

Nanny Mary also prepared all the food for the reception. She is a very talented lady. Cousins May and Sandra also assisted by arranging the tables for the buffet, which was tastefully displayed.

Ruth and Len arrived later for the celebrations. About 50 people joined us for the buffet.

Next Saturday 23rd May, my son Joseph and his wife Maria will leave with the Birmingham Diocese, for their annual Pilgrimage trip to Lourdes.

There is also the Confirmation of Jordan, my great-grandson in Waterford, S. Ireland, on 31st May.

Looking at the beautiful dresses worn by the children today, I remember when Annie, my youngest daughter made her Confirmation at St Osburgs R.C. Church, Coventry in 1961.

The dress that I had purchased in a sale for her was too short. So I bought a few yards of white net in the Coventry Market, pleated, and then stitched it by hand all around the hem of the dress, so it came below the knee.

With the same netting I then made a headdress for her veil, to complete the outfit.

I made ringlets in her long blonde hair, the old fashioned way, with rags. She did look lovely!

Mothers of that time, like me, had to make do, and all their efforts were just as rewarding, as the mothers of today.

This month of May, 2009 was marked by many important family events, such as; Holy Communions, Confirmation, a Wedding Engagement and Birthdays.

A remarkable and memorable way to complete this month.

Annie's Confirmation

Mag' Ist Holy Communion

Annie's Ist Holy Communion

CHAPTER TWELVE

The Malta Trip

Now that summer is near, we can look forward hopefully to some warm weather. A lot of the residents here will be planning their holidays at this time.

Currently, my hospital appointments are preventing me from booking a holiday. I would hope to visit Ireland later in the year. Perhaps September time, which as a rule, weather wise, is a nice month. Also the children are back at school, making travelling easier.

I enjoyed a few holidays on the Island of Malta. The last time was in October 2006, and the weather was beautiful.

Ruth and I sat on the rocks and were enjoying the sun and the view. Eventually it was time for us to move. I was struggling to get up from the sitting position, and I found that I had sat in a puddle of water, with my shorts clinging to my well proportioned posterior.

Unknown to me Ruth had a camera in her bag, and got a perfect picture of me in a very embarrassing position. My face would stop a clock! As we laughed together, Ruth struggled to help me up, and we both fell in a heap.

Wet, battered and bruised, we laughed all the way back to the Hotel.

The following day we decided to go on a bus ride to the beach. What a journey that was, in a bus that was 'out of the ark,' the seats were most uncomfortable.

The driver ignored all the bus stops, and took no notice of peoples request to get off.

Passengers had no chance and no choice. Because of the winding roads, they were being thrown all over the bus.

The bell was a piece of string dangling from overhead, and did not work anyway!

At traffic lights people made the effort to leave the bus, but were told off by the sour-faced conductor.

When the bus reached the terminus, we were allowed to alight. We thanked him for nothing, but unfortunately he did not understand us.

After trudging down the embankment to the beach, we were blown in all directions with the force of the wind. But still we were determined to paddle in the sea.

If we felt suicidal we had an ideal opportunity. We still had to make a return journey, so we climbed the embankment and made our way to the dreaded bus stop.

At last the bus came bumping along. As reluctant as we were we still had to board it.

Well would you believe it? It was only the same conductor! I said, 'Please take us to Bugibba.'

He said, 'No get off and walk, Bugibba, is not very far, me go to Slima. GO!'

We eventually reached the Hotel, in time for our meal. The lift wasn't reliable and it was pot luck if it stopped on the required floor! The twin-bedroom we shared was in the front of the Hotel, facing a noisy Nightclub.

Ruth promptly requested a change of room, and this was granted. The next room was in a better position, overlooking a swimming pool. So we were able to get a good night's sleep.

It was a package holiday, so we just 'went with the flow' and made the most of it.

We visited the lovely Island of Gozo, which involved a coach and ferry journey. Ruth had the misfortune to stumble, and fall down the ramp, which is used for securing rowing boats in rough weather.

As she tripped, she had a surprised and embarrassed expression on her face,

I shouted, 'Where are you going?'

Then I realized then she had hurt her knee but she managed to shrug it off with a laugh.

Making our way back to the coach, all of a sudden Ruth shouted excitedly, 'Billy, Billy!'

'Who's Billy?' I said.

'Billy Connolly the comedian!'

'So, what about him, anyway I'm going to the coach.'

I just kept walking, but Ruth obviously forgetting her bruised knee, had already started running towards this celebrity and was embracing him.

I thought 'My God, what's happening here.'

As I glanced through the window, I saw her being photographed with him. Her face was beaming!

The coach driver asked me where my friend was, as he was waiting to leave.

I said, 'She's with Billy Connolly.'

This incident caused quite a stir, as most of the passengers scrambled to get off the bus to meet this celebrity.

The driver was totally confused!

Anyway, Ruth eventually tore herself away from him joining me on the coach and filled me in on the news.

Apparently, Billy and his family had a home in Gozo.

He recalled that he had met Ruth in 1983 in Rundle Mall in Adelaide, South Australia, where she then lived.

Ruth & Billy

The week's holiday turned out to be amusing, and unusual to say the least!

Malta really is beautiful, so the little drawbacks paled into insignificance, compared with the enjoyment of the holiday.

We appreciated the lovely weather, and people in general where friendly and helpful. Especially the shop assistants, as we wandered around the stores looking at various souvenirs.

On our walks we enjoyed a few lunches in the many restaurants on the Island.

Walking along the beach one day, we decided to have an ice-cream in the nearby café. We were embarrassed when we realized, we had left a trail of sand from our sandals, on their marble floor. However, we were immediately put at ease by the owner.

Our visits to their beautiful Churches will always be memorable. We were reminded by a lady standing at the Church entrance to cover our shoulders, as a sign of modesty, as she handed us a scarf.

We noticed visitors taking photographs of the magnificent surroundings, no doubt to remind them of their holiday in Malta.

The Church were we attended Mass was within walking distance from the hotel, it was small and cosy, and in complete contrast to the larger and more elaborate Churches scattered on the Island.

It was convenient that there were so many nice restaurants by the side of the Church, with several tables outside with parasols. So after Mass we relaxed as we enjoyed a coffee, and just watched people passing by.

Looking back now, we often laugh about our experiences, and even plan another trip to the beautiful Island of Malta.

CHAPTER THIRTEEN

It's Sunday 24th May, a beautiful warm sunny day. I have my windows open and as I write, I can hear the Blackbirds and Sparrows singing away in the leafy trees that adorn the Courtyard, here at Bond's.

The sound of the birds singing is very soothing, and they warble and whistle, they seem to be in harmony with each other.

The singing continues for most of the day, and they never seem to tire! It relaxes me while writing. I imagine myself being in the heart of the country, and not, living as I am, in the middle of a busy City Centre.

The gardens adjoining the flats are looking good now, with all the lovely flowers, such as; roses, clematis, tulips and azalea's, all displaying a blaze of colour.

This is a lovely time of year, and it's hard to imagine that in a few weeks, we will have the longest day, as we then drift slowly into autumn.

This is also a beautiful time of year, when the leaves turn to red and gold and drift past my window, before gently falling to the ground.

However, we still have time to enjoy our gardens and the lawns, which are well groomed by Les, as he cheerfully goes about his work.

The Residents take great pride in their gardens. Their hanging baskets and flower pots are well positioned on their patios.

They can sit and admire the display from their living rooms.

I don't think I would like trying to cope alone in a house now, at this stage of my life.

There is a lot t o be said for Sheltered Accommodation as one gets older. We all seem to have a lot in common here, and we feel safe and secure in our homes. And that is so important.

We have the 'red cord,' which we can pull in any emerg-

ency. This gets you through to Central Control, and they in turn get in touch with the staff that are on call.

They arrive very quickly. Likewise, in the case of an electrical or plumbing fault, this is also dealt with quickly and efficiently.

Any worries we may have can be discussed with the staff, and is of course confidential.

The fire alarm is checked regularly. A few weeks ago I had the misfortune to have my microwave of ten years, cause the alarm to go off about 1.30pm!

Ruth was on the computer at the time and I was preparing lunch. I was heating a small fruit pudding, and low and behold, in a matter of minutes, my apartment was filled with thick black smoke.

Jan and Les were on the scene very quickly, getting Ruth and myself out in case of smoke inhalation.

The Fire Brigade were soon on the scene, and made everything safe. Four or five young men arrived and they were 'drop dead' gorgeous! I was wishing I was 50 years younger! They calmed me down, and were anxious for me to have a check-up at the hospital, but I declined.

Seeing them, and being responsible for the call-out, I don't know which I was more excited about. I forgot about my teenage crush on Robert Taylor!

Jan knocked on my door again before going off duty, and made me promise to pull the cord, should I experience any breathing problems during the night. Thankfully, that was not necessary. All was well.

However, Maisy, a resident aged 91, with an apartment on the ground floor, had the same experience with her microwave, again heating a fruit pudding, that same night at 7pm.

Ruth was just leaving the building on her way home, and she informed me later, that it was the same Firemen attending the scene. Lucky Maisy?

So well done to all you brave, handsome Firemen!

It's times like these that make me grateful I am not living on my own. And when I'm preparing for bed at night, 'a time I enjoy,' having a shower and slipping into my nightie, as I climb into bed very tired, it's comforting to know so many people in the building are doing the same thing.

I include them all in my prayers and ask 'Our Lord' to watch over us and keep us all safe, through the night.

A lot of our residents shop early in the morning. The Co-op in Corporation Street is a popular and convenient store for all of us.

We collect our Pension from the Post Office on the ground floor. The staff are polite and helpful. These girls are also patient and efficient, with a sense of humour.

I remember asking one of the girls, as she weighed my books one morning, 'Do you think they are wrapped securely enough?'

'Securely enough?' she said, 'it would be easier to get into 'Fort Knox'!'

SHARING MY RECIPES

CHAPTER FOURTEEN

Recipes Ofthe 1950'S

SUMMER BRACK

INGREDIENTS

1 lb Flour
½ pint Milk
1 tsp. Ground Ginger
Pinch of salt
4 ozs Margarine
2 heaped tsp. Baking Powder
6 ozs Sugar
6ozs Sultanas
2 sticks of Rhubarb – stewed in 2 tblsp. of water
1 egg

METHOD

1. Pre-heat oven to 180c-350f or gas 4.
2. Sieve flour, salt and baking powder into a bowl.
3. Rub in margarine until it resembles bread crumbs.
4. Mix in sugar, ginger, and sultanas.
5. Finally fold in rhubarb and beaten egg.
6. Pour mixture into a greased and lined 9 inch tin or dish and bake in pre-heated oven for 1.3/4 hours.

BOILED FRUIT CAKE

Line a 6-inch cake tin with greased-proof paper. Set aside; turn on the oven to moderate heat 360f/ gas mark 4.

8 ozs S.R. Flour
½ level tsp. of Nutmeg.
Level tsp. Mixed Spice.
Pinch of Salt.
4 ozs Soft Margarine
6ozs Sultanas or Mixed Fruit.
4 ozs Sugar.
12 tablespoons of water
Sieve all dry ingredients in mixing bowl.

Put sugar, margarine, fruit and water in a saucepan. Stir over low heat until margarine is melted and sugar is dissolved. Bring to the boil, lower heat again and simmer for 3 mins. Allow to cool to lukewarm, quickly stir in ½ level tsp. bicarb. of soda. Make well in centre of flour and dry ingredients. Pour in cooled mixture from the saucepan. Stir quickly, mixing thoroughly. Turn into prepared tin and smooth the top.

Bake on the middle shelf for 1hr.15mins. Remove from oven. Test cake is cooked by inserting knife into centre, making sure it comes out dry. Turn onto a wire tray and allow to cool. When cold, this cake is a good standby and keeps well in an air-tight tin.

OLD-FASHIONED BREAD PUDDING

INGREDIENTS

Small stale loaf
6 Ozs of Raisins, Sultanas or Mixed fruit.
3 Dessertspoons of sugar
2 Tsp of mixed spice
2 ozs of margarine
1 egg
1 med sized sq. tin /oven proof dish, greased well with butter for better flavour.

METHOD

Pre-heat oven to moderate
Soak bread in cold water for 30 mins. Then Squeeze out the liquid. Transfer to mixing bowl. Melt margarine and pour into bread mixture. Add sugar and mixed spice, stir with a wooden spoon. Beat egg and add, with fruit to mixture. Beat well.
Transfer mixture into prepared dish or tin, smooth the top, and sprinkle with granulated or brown sugar. Bake on the middle shelf for about 1 hour.
Then allow to cool in container. Cut into squares.
Serve cold or hot, with custard or cream or on its own. This pudding is also delicious steamed for 2-1/2 to 3 hours.

IRISH CHESTER BREAD

Ingredients for pastry.
6 ozs of S.R. flour
3ozs of hard margarine
2 Tablespoon of cold water

Cut in the margarine with a knife and mix with fingers until it resembles fine breadcrumbs. Add about 2 tablespoons of water. Mix with a fork until bowl is clean. Turn onto floured board. Shape pastry into a ball, and allow to stand in fridge for about 30 mins.

Butter an 8 inch tin or oven proof dish (set aside)
Cut the refrigerated pastry in half; roll out ½ to line the tin.

FOR FILLING

Fill the tin with previous recipe for bread pudding mixture. Roll out remaining pastry and cover. Seal edges with a fork and brush with milk or beaten egg.

Bake in a pre-heated (fairly hot) oven for about ¾ hr depending on oven temperature. Cut into squares, this recipe keeps well.

ROCK CAKES OR BUNS

Prepare a baking sheet by brushing all over with soft margarine. Turn on the oven, setting it to fairly hot (Gas Mark 6) or (400 F.).

INGREDIENTS

8 ozs S.R. Flour
Pinch of salt
3ozs Margarine
3 ozs Sugar
3-4ozs Sultanas or Mixed Fruit
3 dessertspoons of Milk
1 Egg

METHOD

Sieve flour and salt together in a bow. Rub in 3ozs margarine, stir 3ozs sugar into the mixture with a metal spoon and add 3-4ozs of Sultanas or Mixed Fruit. Beat the egg lightly with the milk, add to the mixture and stir thoroughly together. Place heaped dessertspoons of the mixture in rough heaps, a little apart on the coated baking sheet. Place on middle shelf of the pre-heated oven for 20 -25 minutes. Remove the cakes from the baking sheet and cool on a wire tray. Makes 10-12 cakes.

SODA BREAD

INGREDIENTS

12. ozs Wholemeal flour
4 ozs White flour
2 Tablespoons of Bran
1 Tablespoon wheat-germ
1 tsp Bicarbonate of soda
½ tsp Salt
1egg
2ozs Butter
½ pint of Buttermilk

METHOD

Sieve white flour and wheat-germ into a bowl; fold in the wholemeal flour and bran. Add soda and salt. Rub in the butter. Make a well in the centre of the flour and add beaten egg and butter milk. Mix to a fairly loose dough, knead lightly, and form into a cake, making a cross on top.
Flour a baking tray and place on the middle shelf in a fairly hot oven, 425f (Gas mark 5) for about 45minutes.

ALL-IN-ONE FARMHOUSE FRUIT CAKE

INGREDIENTS

6 ozs Soft Margarine
6 ozs Castor Sugar
8 ozs Self Raising Flour * * Sieve together
½ Level tsp Mixed Spice *
½ Teaspoon salt *
3 Eggs (large)
10 ozs Sultanas or Mixed dried fruit
2 oz Glazed Cherries (halved)
2 oz Mixed peel

METHOD

Place all ingredients together in a mixing bowl and beat with a wooden spoon until well mixed (2-3 minutes). Place in a greased and lined 7 in round cake tin. Smooth top, bake in a preheated very moderate oven (325f - Gas mark 3) on middle shelf for 1.1/2- 1.3/4hrs. Leave in tin for 2-3 minutes then turn out, cool on wire tray.

ALL IN ONE APPLE SPONGE

(Preheat oven to 425f. or Gas mark 5)

8 ozs S.R. Flour
6 ozs Sugar (preferably brown)
6 ozs Soft Margarine
2 Large Eggs
2 tsps. Of Cinnamon
3 ozs Sultanas
1 Large Bramley Cooking Apple (cored, peeled and finely chopped)

METHOD

Put all dry ingredients into a large bowl. Add margarine, and chopped apple.
Add sultanas to mixture, then add beaten eggs and if necessary, a little milk. Using a wooden spoon, stir well.
Butter an 8-10 inch oven proof dish. Place mixture into prepared dish. Cook for about 1 hour, according to oven temperature.

Serve warm with cream
This sponge keeps well and is a good stand-by.
*This is my favourite recipe.

IRISH POTATO STUFFING

INGREDIENTS

3 Large Potatoes
1 Medium Onion
½ oz Butter
1 or 2 Tsp Mixed Herbs (according to taste)
Pinch of Salt and Pepper
A little Milk

METHOD

Peel the potatoes, cut small, bring to the boil in a little water and simmer for about 20 minutes.
Strain the water off; add the finally chopped onion and butter. Mash well until smooth. Then add salt, pepper, mixed herbs and a dash of milk. (If required).

This stuffing can be put in a dish and baked in a fairly hot oven until brown, and forms a nice crust, or placed inside the bird, or as an accompaniment for pork. If used in poultry, as a stuffing, increase the cooking time of the bird to ensure it's thoroughly cooked and juices run clear. Always allow stuffing to get cold, (never use hot stuffing in fresh, uncooked meat).

IRISH POTATO CAKES

(ALSO KNOWN AS BOXTY)

1lb Potatoes (cooked and mashed while still warm)
4 ozs Flour
1 oz Butter
Salt and Pepper
A little Milk
Oil, Butter or Lard for frying

METHOD

Put mashed potatoes in a large bowl with salt and pepper, butter and milk. Work the flour in gradually, mixing to a smooth dough, adding more flour if necessary. Divide into 2 rounds, each about ¼ inches thick. Cut into tri-angles.

Have the pan or griddle nicely hot. Grease well. Cook the cakes on both sides until golden brown.
Add more oil, butter or lard as you cook, to prevent sticking. Serve hot with butter or with bacon and eggs.
(This is an ideal way to use up left over potatoes)

This recipe makes 10-14 potato cakes – enjoy.

THE CLOSING

It has been a long journey since September, 2006 when I launched my first book; 'Five Children, Five Cases, Five Pounds,' relating the memories of my childhood and growing up in Waterford, Southern Ireland.

It was a painful book to pen, but it was also therapeutic and no doubt it has helped me along the way.

I have been told by the Library, it has had a high readership, along with my other two books; 'River Factory Tales' and 'Never Had It So Good.'

They have also sold well, both here and in Ireland. It is rewarding when people express how much they enjoyed my books, and most had their own reasons.

It was common for some to say,

'I cried all the way through your first book.'

Others said, 'I laughed and cried.'

Comments regarding 'River Factory Tales' included,

'What a lovely gentle book.' And 'Weren't you the little demon?'

Nearly all could identify with the stories, but at least I stirred up emotions. And I'm told that's what a book is all about.

I'm not a great reader myself. I can lose concentration, unless the stories hold my interest. However, I do admire fiction writers; I think they are very clever.

Personally, I have to experience what I write about. But who knows what tomorrow may bring? Perhaps I will be inspired again?

I'm sure there wasn't anything unusual or heroic about my life, except maybe, I can never remember being really happy.

Whatever that may mean?

My parents and my Grandmother were huge figures in my life. They instilled in me a faith in God, and my Catholic education also helped me greatly, through the ups and downs along the rough road!

For some years now, I have been absorbed in a world of books and remembering. I do feel sad I have now reached the end of writing. It's like losing a friend!

Although I did say it was the closing of the biography in my last book, the opportunity arose with the evacuation at Bonds. This inspired me once more, to write and 'move with the muse.'

Expressing myself at times was hard, and getting it all to flow into stories.

It is said, people do love to read about other people. I hope somebody, someday, somewhere, will learn something from what I have written; my mistakes, the silly times, the sad and painful experiences.

The loneliness of having been cut off from reality, while going through the 'tunnel,' which at times was very long, but eventually I did glimpse the light and struggled on!

I'm happy to say my family emerged quite well from the turmoil. I love them all very much, and did what any responsible mother would do. I won't get any medals for that, it was my duty.

Through the traumatic times I needed them, as much as they needed me. It was my children who made it all worthwhile. Like most families they often made me cry, but they certainly made me laugh too.

I feel my work is now complete and the struggle over. It was a long haul, but I still have all my faculties? Shhhh!

I get about fairly well, if a little slower.

There is one lady I see often in the street, as I'm shopping. She is very frail, almost bent over, depending on her walking frame for support. What courage she portrays. I wonder what her life story would be.

The meaning of life is explained so well in some of the old songs.

One that stands out very much in my mind is 'Smoke Gets in Your Eyes.' I think it explains our mistakes.

It's fair to say, perhaps, this book brings you 'all kinds of everything to remind you of me!

As I reflect and ponder over the years, all my stories now seem like fairy tales that I once read about.

SOME OF MY FAVOURITE SONGS

Here are a few songs to send my book on its way. Some are special to me. Here's hoping you're in good voice?

Sweet Sixteen

When I first saw the love light in your eyes,
And heard your voice in sweetest melody,
Speak words of love to my enraptured soul,
The world had nought but joy in store for me;
But now we're drifting down life's stream apart,
Your dear kind face I see in dreams' domain,
I know that it would ease my aching heart,
To hold you in my arms just once again.

<u>CHORUS</u>
I love you as I never loved before,
Since first I met you on the village green;
Come to me ere my dream of love is o'er,
I love you as I loved you, when you were sweet -
When you were sweet sixteen.

Last night I dreamt I held your hand in mine,
And once again you were my happy bride;
I kissed you as I did in auld lang syne,
As from the church we wandered side by side,
My love for you will never, never die,
Without you I would rather not be born,
And tho' we two may never meet again,
I love you as the sunshine loves the morn.

<u>CHORUS</u>

Maggie

I wandered to-day to the hill, Maggie,
To watch the scene below;
The creek and the old rustic mill, Maggie,
Where we sat in the long, long ago,
The green grove is gone from the hill, Maggie,
Where first the daisy's sprung,
The old rustic mill is still, Maggie,
Since you and I were young.

A city so silent and lone, Maggie,
Where the young and the gay and the best,
In polished white mansions of stone, Maggie,
Have each found a place of rest,
It's built where the birds used to play, Maggie
And join in the songs that were sung;
For we sang just as gay as they, Maggie
When you and I were young.

They say I am feeble with age, Maggie,
My steps are less sprightly than then;
My face is a well-written page, Maggie,
But time alone was the pen;
They say we are aged and grey, Maggie,
As spray in the white breakers flung,
But to me you're as fair as you were, Maggie,
When you and I were young.

And now we are aged and grey, Maggie,
The trials of life nearly done;
Let us sing of the days that are gone, Maggie
When you and I were young.

Liverpool Lou

I go a-walking hear people talking,
School children playing.
I know what they're saying.
They're saying you'll grieve me,
That you will deceive me,
Some morning you'll leave me,
All packed up and gone.

<u>CHORUS</u>
Oh, Liverpool Lou, lovely Liverpool Lou,
Why don't you behave just like other girls do?
Why must my poor heart keep following you?
Stay home and love me, my Liverpool Lou.

The sounds from the river keep telling me ever
That I should forget you, like I never met you.
Tell me their song, love, was never more wrong love.
Say I belong, love, to my Liverpool Lou.

<u>CHORUS</u>

Sunshine Of Your Smile

Dear face that holds so sweet a smile for me,
Were you not mine how dark this world would be?
I know no light above that can replace
loves radiant sunshine,
In your dear, dear face.

Give me your smile the love light in your eyes,
Life could not hold a fairer paradise,
Give me the right to love you all the while,
My world forever,
The sunshine of your smile.

Shadows may fall across the land and sea,
Sunshine from all this world may hidden be,
But I shall see no cloud across the sun,
Your smile shall light my way 'til life is done.
Give me your smile, the love light in your eyes,
My world forever.
The sunshine of your smile.

Scarlet Ribbons

I peeped in to say good night,
When I heard my child in prayer,
'Send, dear god, some scarlet ribbons,
Scarlet ribbons for my hair.'

All the stores were closed and shuttered,
All the streets were dark and bare.
In our town no scarlet ribbons,
Not one ribbon for her hair.

Through the night my heart was aching.
Just before the dawn was breaking,
I peeped in and on her bed
In gay profusion lying there,
I saw ribbons, scarlet ribbons,
Scarlet ribbons for her hair.

Though I live to be a hundred,
I will never know from where
Came those ribbons, scarlet ribbons,
Scarlet ribbons for her hair.

This song is very close to my heart. It was popular when my baby son Noel died, and the words also remind me of my beloved daughter Mary Catherine. She laughed her way through life.

I Shall Always Remember You Smiling

I shall always remember you smiling,
In my tenderest memories of you,

All alone how I try to keep smiling,
In a way that you'd want me to do,

And if ever you need me,
As I'm needing you,

I shall hear if you whisper my name,
I shall always remember you smiling,

You'll be smiling when we meet again.

Any Dream Will Do

I closed my eyes, drew back the curtain,
To see for certain what I thought I knew,
Far, far away, someone was weeping,
But the world was sleeping,
Any dream will do.

I wore my coat with golden lining,
Bright colours shining, wonderful and new.
And in the east, the dawn was breaking,
And the world was waking,
Any dream will do.

Chorus

A crash of drums, a flash of light,
My golden coat flew out of sight,
Colours faded into darkness,
I was left alone.
May I return, to the beginning.
The light is dimming, and the dream is too.
The world and I, we are still waiting,
Still hesitating, any dream will do.

(Repeat chorus again).

This is a tribute to my home town WATERFORD

My City Of Music

My city of music, won't you play a song I can remember,
To take with me wherever I may wander,
Far from this ancient city that I love.

My city of music, let me hear the sound of song and laughter,
And leave with me a memory ever after,
Of pleasant days beside your river shore.

No matter where I wander, no matter where I roam,
I see your lights before me; they're calling me back home.
Your quayside and your lane-ways,
They never seem to change,
Your ways and old traditions, don't ever rearrange.

My city of music, won't you play a song I can remember,
To take with me wherever I may wander,
Far from this ancient city that I love.

My city of music, let me hear the sound of song and
laughter,
And leave with me a memory ever after,
Of pleasant days beside your river shore,

My City of Music continued:

The sunny Sunday mornings, listening to the band,
The look on children's faces, who don't quite understand.

The sound of church bells ringing, seem to fill the air,
Choir's softly singing,
There's nothing to compare,
To my city of music,
Won't you play a song I can remember,
To take with me wherever I may wander,
Far from this ancient city that I love.

My city of music, won't you play a song I can remember,
To take with me wherever I may wander,
Far from this ancient city that I love.
My city of music,
Let me hear the sound of song and laughter,
And leave with me a memory ever after,
Of pleasant days beside your river shore.

My city of music won't you play a song for me.
This version of the song is by Richie Hayes. (Waterford)

When A Child Is Born

A ray of hope flickers in the sky,
A tiny star lights up way up high.
All across the land dawns a brand-new morn,
This comes to pass,
When a child is born.

A silent wish sails the seven seas,
The winds of change whisper in the trees,
And the wall of doubt crumbles tossed and torn.
This comes to pass,
When a child is born.

A rosy hue settles all around.
You've got the feel you're on solid ground.
For a spell or two no one seems forlorn.
This comes to pass
When a child is born.

When A Child Is Born Continues:

Spoken
And all this happens
Because the world is waiting,
Waiting for one child.
Black, white, yellow,
No one knows,
But a child that will grow up
And turn tears to laughter,
Hate to love, war to peace
And everyone to everyone's
Neighbour,
And misery and suffering
Will be worlds
To be forgotten forever.

Sung
It's all a dream,
An illusion now.
It must come true
Sometimes soon somehow.
All across the land
Dawns a brand-new morn.
This comes to pass
When a child is born.

Sharing Love

Have you a song within your heart,
Have you a smile to share?
Have you a moment in the day
To show someone you care?
Have you the time to be a friend
And listen when they call?
Have you the courage every day
To step out, walking tall?

Have you a hope for all mankind
Whatever faith or creed?
Have you the strength to show the way
To those who are in need?
If you've a song, a smile, a hope,
A special dream or two,
You have discovered love, my friend,
And love discovered you!

Poem by Iris Hesselden

SYNOPSIS

The recession plus the discovery of an unexploded German bomb in Coventry, March 08; prompted Brigid once again to continue her stories of the 40's and 50's.

Another opportunity arose, and inspired her to travel back, remembering, as she reveals two different worlds in values and morality; and comparing the struggles of families, striving to make ends meet back then, with the modern 'selfish' attitude of today; 'We want it all and we want it now!'

So perhaps the recession we currently find ourselves in, is a blessing in disguise!

ABOUT THE AUTHOR

Brigid Patricia Boggan was born in Waterford, Southern Ireland in 1925.

She now resides in Coventry, United Kingdom.

This is the fourth and final book of her Biography. Brigid published her first book in September, 2006.

Other titles are;

Five Children, Five Cases, Five Pounds

River Factory Tales

Never Had It So Good

VERY SPECIAL THANKS

Ruth Cattell - my dear friend for her consistency and dedication in co-editing and typing my books. Her sense of humour was much appreciated.

Len Cattell - for his photographic work.

My Son Billy – for the cover design.

William – for his patience in correcting and proof reading.

My granddaughter and godchild, Deborah – for all her help with Launches and book distributions.

My daughter Mags for the Launch Catering and all her hard work

My daughter Annie for her skill and hard work in re-designing my apartment

Cousin Paul and Peg – for keeping in touch

Children and Grandchildren

Relations in Waterford and Tramore – for being there

Sending best wishes to my Godson and cousin, in the U.S.A.

Tom Falconer – for entertaining us with his music

Maggie Gallagher and her Dance Team

Mo in Spain

Phil and Staff at Waterstones, Cathedral Lanes

Irish Society

Irish Post

The Harp

Book Centre Waterford - for all your efforts

The Granary Museum, The Quay – for your interest

My Readers scattered far and wide – for your many cards and letters.

Special thanks to Mr Keene, our Chairman at Bonds – for speaking so well on my behalf, at my book Launches.